Love, Laughter
and
Our Long Goodbye

Grandma's story and mine

KRISTEN HARTMAN

For Grandma—I love you, I love you, I love you.

ACKNOWLEDGMENTS

My grandma, Maxine Dagen, was loved and lost by many, and each could write a book of the time they shared with her, but I can only write the story the two of us penned in our times together. Any inaccuracies or oversights are mine alone.

Deepest thanks to my family:
Mom, Dad, Jon and **Kevin**—I am the most blessed girl in the world to have you for parents and big brothers.
Angela and **Wendy**—thank you for loving my brothers so well and being the sisters I always wanted.
Kayla, Aaron, Norah and **Lauren**—you had the most amazing great-grandma! You may not remember her (Lauren, I wish you could have met her), but I promise I'll tell you all about her.
Uncle Brian, Aunt Jill, Jess and **Amy**—I love being yours.
Grandpa—thank you for loving Grandma and all of us. I love you!

My fabulous **Ignight family**, and many **treasured friends**, who prayed me through these months and beyond—
thank you, thank you, thank you.

Jenni and **Mike**—thank you for believing in my words long before I believed in them. I struck gold when I entered your classrooms, and I'm grateful beyond words that you continue to make me a better writer.

Each who loved and cared for Grandma, those who visited, sent cards, called and loved her and all of us—I am humbled by your presence in her life and mine.

PROLOGUE

"Grandma, tell me a story."

Those words slipped out of my mouth hundreds—maybe thousands—of times. I loved listening to Grandma dip into her childhood almost six decades before my own. I loved the stories she spun about games of tag in the cornfield, collecting eggs in the chicken coop, stoking the fire in the one-room schoolhouse and dancing with her brothers on Saturday nights at the Grange Hall. I never tired of her stories.

Grandma was born in a farmhouse in western Michigan on May 26, 1924. She was the youngest of John and Emma Borgman's nine children, and though she left the farm when she was eighteen it was never more than a memory away. She lived her adult life in cities and suburbs—and mostly thousands of miles away from her family— but when I asked for a story, we were back on the farm. I heard about her parents, her four older brothers and four older sisters, the chores, the traditions, the jokes and the heartaches. Sometimes I asked for and received stories about her early years in California, about her marriage to my mom's father or about the pranks she pulled on her bosses and friends. I treasured those stories, too, but the farm was the formative factor of Grandma's life and, in many ways, of my life.

I am built on her foundation. My love of words is rooted in the fertile soil of Michigan farm country, and our stories can never be shaken free of the ground in which they were nourished.

But I didn't know how stunning it would be when the phone call came that we'd entered a new chapter of our lives—that Grandma might be writing the last pages of her story. I didn't know how many tears I would shed on the pages as we turned them together.

So . . . this is a chronicle of the hardest goodbye I've ever said.

Many days I left Grandma's side and sat in my car scribbling teary transcripts of our conversations or went home and pounded my grief into a keyboard because I knew I couldn't bear to forget any of it—but neither could I trust my memory to hold it—so I wrote and I wrote and I wrote.

I didn't know how many chances I'd have to hold her hand and whisper, "Grandma, tell me a story."

OUR STORY

Sunday, January 12

I stand in the doorway and watch. She hasn't seen me yet. Inside the hospital room is my grandma.

As I gaze at her I wonder if the nurses and doctors can see what I see. Can they see beyond the ailments attacking her body and mind to who she really is?

I see what they see. I see the scoliosis-wracked spine that's tilted her forward and to the right. I see the eye that's never recovered from the acute narrow angle glaucoma attack. I hear the dry, rattling cough that may or may not be related to the pneumonia rampaging through both of her scar-tissue riddled lungs. I see the flush of fever across her cheeks. I hear the lucidity wax and wane. I see how much gown there is to cover her ever-shrinking frame.

I do.

But that 89-year old body is not my grandma.

No, this woman who tells me she will miss us all, but she is ready to go—she is ready for God to take her home—this is, but so isn't, my grandma.

My grandma is the woman thanking her nurses and calling them "honey." She is the woman cracking jokes to diffuse the pain of uncertain times . . . even as she struggles to grasp her present reality.

She is the woman who sang "There is a tavern in the town" to me countless times because I love the story of the song. And I love imagining it tying tight the generations: her father sang it to her, she sang it to my mom while they drove cross-country to restart their lives alone and she sang it to me in her unmistakable alto every time I asked for years.

I wish I could ask her to sing it right now. I know the words are still inside her. I want to hear them. I want to hear all her words— all the stories—again. I want to ask the questions and hear the answers again and again, but I can't. Now when I want so badly to hear her voice, I have to encourage her to be quiet and rest to try to give her lungs a chance to recover.

So I tell the stories to myself. As I sit next to her and cool her forehead with my hands, I picture myself at her kitchen table, eating my umpteenth molasses cookie and asking for stories. And in my head I listen to her tell them once more . . .

It was my job to collect the eggs from the chicken coop. We probably had thirty chickens at any time. The eggs fed the family, and Mother also sold them to bring in some money. But I hated it. I was afraid of the chickens—they pecked my hands and arms when I reached under them for the eggs. They were so mean. (My favorite days were when Mother would send Johnny and me to go get a chicken for Sunday dinner. One less chicken.) I hurried through the giant coop as quickly as I could. Then one summer day racing to get out of the coop, I tripped and the pail of eggs went flying. Almost all of the eggs were broken. Afraid I would get in trouble, I hid the broken eggs under the back stoop. I gave Mother the few remaining eggs and told her it was a bad laying day. I'm sure she didn't believe me, but she didn't say anything. Of course, the eggs began to rot in the heat, and I couldn't do anything about the stench. I was found out.

Somehow in my mind that good story is still tied to one of the worst stories. Grandma was the youngest of nine children. The eldest was nineteen when she was born. When Grandma was six, one of her older sisters gave their mother a trip to visit a relative. Grandma and her next oldest sister Bernice, who was ten, were alone in the kitchen. As Bernice banked the wood-burning stove, her coat caught on fire. She didn't know what to do, so she ran. Grandma chased her. An older sister heard their screams and smothered the flames. Bernice lingered for three days before dying. Their parents never once discussed her death. Decades later it haunted Grandma that she never thought to ask her mother how she was feeling on Bernice's birthday or other significant days.

I loved having a big family. On the weekends when my brothers and sisters would come home from their jobs, I'd check my brothers' front pockets for candy. It wasn't always there, but often it was.

They would go out to the Grange Hall for dances. Usually round or square dancing. There wasn't a lot of entertainment out in the country—life revolved around the Grange. And they'd always take me along. They couldn't leave me at home by myself. We lived in a big farmhouse. And I would have had to take that lantern upstairs by myself—Mom wouldn't let me do that. My dad was the chairman of the committee. He and Mom sold the refreshments, like a slice of cake and coffee. They had other people who helped them. I didn't dance. I just watched. One night my brother Bill came up and asked me to dance, and I said, "Oh no, I don't know how to dance!" And he said, "I'll teach you." So we danced. I couldn't wait for the next school day to go tell my little friends I knew how to dance. I'm sure I didn't really know how to dance at all, but I was so proud.

As the youngest child Grandma's life was a little different from her older siblings' lives. She didn't have quite as many chores on the farm, and she was often spoiled by her brothers and sisters. The youngest boy, John, was twelve when Grandma was born. He was the only one who stayed on the farm when he reached adulthood.

If the boys had stayed on the farm like they should have, it probably would have been a good farm . . . but it was hard to be a farmer. John stayed too long. He got nothing for it. Monetarily. It was hard to make a go. I loved being on the farm. But my brother, Byron, paid for me to go to business college, so I could get a good job. I went to Muskegon Business College for one year.

I lived with my sister Verlyn and her husband Alvin, and when I had a ride I'd go to the farm for the weekend. They lived maybe ten blocks from the school, so I mostly walked. Alvin had a grocery store and after we got done with work— or school for me—we'd go work in the store, too.

When I finished school I got a job in the office at the defense plant. This man, Al, worked in the plant, and he'd give me a ride to work. He was a character right out of the newspaper. He could have been in comedy. He drove a truck, but it just had one seat, so I rode on a crate in the back. I slid all over. It was during the war and there were rations, so I wore leg makeup en lieu of hose. But, oh gosh, I'd slide all over the back of that truck—I looked like I had runs in my fake hose. I'd go into the bathroom and smooth them out.

When Grandma was a young girl, most of her brothers were already working in town, and John did much of the fieldwork on the 40-acre farm. Grandma always wanted to help. She would ride along with him while he plowed and make believe she was plowing. One day when she was around eleven she decided to surprise him. John was out in the east pasture, so she tried to disc the other field. The disc plow had four big round metal discs that rotated through the soil to break it up and prepare it for planting. When John saw the horses out in the field not moving but not where they should have been, he knew something was wrong. He called for their mother to get the doctor as he ran to the field. Somehow Grandma got caught by one of the discs when she tried to start plowing and her legs were badly cut. She never complained, but the leg that got the worst of it still ached decades later from not healing right.

Grandma's parents never learned to drive. They owned vehicles their sons drove, and by the time she was twelve Grandma had learned to drive. Until eighth grade the children went to the   one-room schoolhouse—McNitt School—on the edge of their property. But the nearest high school was about four miles away in Ravenna. Most of her siblings chose to leave school after eighth grade to start working in factories or for town families. Only her brothers Byron and John had finished high school. But Grandma wanted to go to school. She and her friends walked each way to Ravenna unless a passing farmer gave them a ride.

One day Mr. Graftema came by to speak with Dad. He worked for Muskegon County and drove the road grader, but he was going to be away for about a week. He asked Dad if I might want to drive the road grader to school while he was gone. Dad turned to me and asked, "Sister, do you think you can drive it?"

I said, "I think so."

Mr. Graftema left it at our house for me. So every day I'd pick up his daughter—she was two and a half years younger than me—and drive to school. All the boys thought it was so funny. They'd hear us coming and run out to the road and jump on. By the time I'd get to school I hardly had a seat left for me there were so many hanging off the grader.

Wednesday, January 15

It's hard to leave at night. It's hard to leave Grandma alone in a great big hospital room when we know she won't push the call button—even if she remembers it's there—because she never wants to bother anyone. If she wakes up, she'll just lie there and wait for someone to come. And she'll wonder where we are.

Some days my prayers are thoughtfully constructed with great attention to each word and grammatical structure. They're crafted. They're deliberate.

And some days they're no-holds-barred, heart-to-lips-do-not-pass-brain outpourings.

Today is one of those days.

They are thoughtless prayers. Not without care, but without thought. They come from my depths, not from my intellect. I'm not thinking. I'm praying.

I pray without planning to pray. The jumbled words and emotions and fragmentary phrases of petition and praise become one incessant prayer while I work, while I walk, while I carry on conversation, while I eat.

When life jars me and I'm powerless and vulnerable, my normal prayers never get off the ground. They're completely overwhelmed by the instinctual, untrained, natural-as-breathing communication flowing to the very One who designed me to be in constant communion.

With a fragile but fighting heart I begin to grasp praying without ceasing. And it's not some hyper-spiritual, haloed, so full-of-faith-nothing-can-touch-it thing. It's not passive and removed from life. It's active. It's visceral.

I have a moment-by-moment awareness of my great need and great inadequacy commingled with unshakeable confidence that regardless of how my prayers are answered they are being attended to by the greatest physician, wisest counselor, strongest defender, ablest protector, tenderest comforter.

And unlike the days and prayers when I struggle to engage in the dialogue—when it feels more like I'm spouting a soliloquy to an audience of none that echoes back silence—on days like today there is a presence I cannot deny. I am heard. And while the answers are not audible, they are everywhere . . . in the snippets of scripture that come to mind, in the unexpected hug from a friend, in the peace that cradles my cracking heart.

So here I am. Spilling out my fractured, unedited self and words because there is no time—or need—for polish and perfection with the God who knows my thoughts more intimately than I ever will.

Heading to the comfort of home when Grandma can't go home feels wrong. How does she keep fighting when she isn't even sure what she's fighting for in those long minutes of the night?

"Where's that verse: I set before you life and death, choose life?" Mom asked.

"Uhhhh, Deuteronomy. Let me look . . . Deuteronomy 30:19."

"Can you read it to me?"

I found it and read, "'This day I call the heavens and the earth as witnesses against you that I have set before you life and death, blessings and curses. Now choose life, so that you and your children may live'—and then it keeps going in 20."

"That's what I'm praying. I'm praying for her to choose life. And I'm praying for us to choose life for her."

Thursday, January 16

As the days in the hospital passed and the coughing subsided, it became easier for Grandma to talk. I'd pull the heavy chair as close to her bed as I could get it, perch right on the edge and lean in as close as I could to her. And we'd talk. I'd ask for stories or just meander with her through the years and people.

"Grandma, tell me about when you started drinking your coffee black."

"*Oh, I was sharing an apartment with my sister, Sally, and one morning I went to get my coffee and there was no cream. I knew she went to the store the day before, so I said, 'Where's the cream?'*

"*And she said she didn't buy any.*

"*And I said, 'What will I do?'*

"*She said, 'You'll learn.'*

"It broke my heart . . . I drank my coffee black that day."

"So Aunt Sally drank black coffee?"

"Yes. The cream was just for me."

I remembered how Grandma had started drinking coffee as a young girl. Her mom would give her a cup of coffee with cream—or rather a cup of cream with coffee—to warm her up when it was cold. Learning to drink it black as a twenty-year old after years of rich, creamy coffee must have been a shocker.

Sunday, January 19

Jon came down Friday afternoon—the day Kevin's son, her first great-grandson, was born—to spend the weekend with Grandma. He's always been a model grandchild. Though he's lived four hundred miles away for a dozen years, he calls Grandma and Grandpa every week. And when his daughter was born almost two years ago he taught Grandpa to make video calls on Skype so they could see and talk to their long-distance great-granddaughter every week. As Grandma's comfort and ability to carry on a phone conversation have declined, Jon realized mornings are better for her, so sometimes he calls while he's driving to work to chat with her.

This morning I was thinking about Grandma. I'm always thinking about Grandma, but I was thinking about what makes her uniquely her. She has this amazing ability to be present. Somehow I'd missed it until now. She is fully in a moment, and she is fully present to whoever is with her. The person with her has her undivided attention and love. Talking to Grandma is like being the only person in the world—she makes you feel that special. It's a gift. She is right there—not thinking about someone or something else, not planning her own response—wholly present. And somehow it has helped her survive circumstances that would have defeated most anyone else.

Jon got to the hospital first today for some one-on-one time: Grandma and eldest grandchild. Words don't appear on command, and the ones we want to say aren't always the ones that come out. But in the quiet of the morning, they said what they needed, what they could. As the day went on, we all trickled in and joined them.

At one point Grandpa was in my chair. I stood at the foot of the bed while the nurse electronically updated her chart. In mid comment Grandma referred to Grandpa in the third person. She said to him, *"Maybe tomorrow Art and the two guys would like to watch the game."*

He leaned forward, "Do you know my name?"

"Of course I know your name, Honey."

"What is it?"

"Jeffrey."

The nurse froze, hand hovering over the keyboard. Grandpa glared. I bit my lip.

And then—maintaining her straight face—Grandma sighed and murmured, *"Art."*

Grandma and I shared a quick smile as the nurse erupted in laughter and said, "Oh my! I see you still have your sense of humor!" Grandpa was less amused.

By mid-afternoon it was time for Jon to say goodbye. He fought to hold back the tears as he told her how much he loved her.

And then Grandma started to cry.

"You have to go? We had a good two days, didn't we?"

"We did," was all he could manage.

He hugged her and they whispered their last private words before he went to the door and tore off his gown and gloves. Stuffing them in the trash, he struggled to stay composed. Outside the door he peered back through the window and waved before turning away and losing the battle.

Monday, January 20—Martin Luther King, Jr. Day

Last night must have been a long one. Her eyes kept searching our faces this morning as she'd quietly repeat, *"I thought I'd lost you. I thought I'd never see you again."*

Mom and I held her hands and reassured her again and again we'd always come back. Every day. We'd always come back.

Mom stepped away to answer the phone, and as I stroked Grandma's hand I said again, "Grandpa is here all day. He comes every morning, and he stays all day. He only goes home at night to eat and sleep. And then he comes right back."

"*And you?*"

"And I come when I get off work. And on the weekends. Mom comes. Uncle Brian comes almost every day. Jessica and Amy will be here this afternoon. Someone is always here, Grandma. We only leave at night."

"*Oh.*"

"We're just not here at night."

"*Have you tried?*"

I blinked hard and squeezed her hand. How could I answer? I'd asked about staying—but had I tried? When she attempted to get out of bed at night, was she looking for us? Was she feeling abandoned? Could she remember at two in the morning why she was alone?

"I asked . . ." I murmured and let it go.

"Grandma, who was it that called the cows? Was that you?"

"*No, that was Dollie. She could get every cow in the county.*"

"Well, if I were a cow, I wouldn't mess with Aunt Dollie. I mean, I wouldn't mess with her anyway."

"*She was spunky. I don't know how she got away with things, but she did. They asked Mother if Dollie would play the piano for the school production. When Mother asked her, she said no.*"

"Did your mom make her play anyway?"

"*She couldn't. Dollie wouldn't do it.*"

"How did she get the cows to come?"

"*She'd kind of cup her hands together like this . . . and then make this opening between her thumbs . . . and then she kind of blew between her thumbs— like a whistling sound—and those cows would lift their heads up and just start coming in.*"

"How many cows?"

"*Let me see. We probably had about 40 at that point.*"

"Forty?!? She'd call forty cows?"

"*Yes. We had to bring them in to be milked. They got angry if you left them out too long.*"

"But you didn't milk them."

"*Oh no. I couldn't do it. I tried, but I just couldn't. I could strip them after they were milked, but I never could milk them."*

As I got ready to leave I leaned close. With our foreheads pressed together I whispered, "I love you, I love you, I love you."

"I love you . . . I love you . . . I love you."

"I'll see you tomorrow. There's nowhere I'd rather be than with you."

"You're my girl."

"I am your girl. I've always been yours, and I always will be."

She squeezed my hand as I kissed her forehead.

Tuesday, January 21

This afternoon Gloria and Glen called from Michigan. Gloria was Grandma's girl when she was little. Her second niece. Grandma loved to take care of Gloria and her older sister, Marlene, when she lived with their parents, Verlyn and Alvin. Seventy years later it's Gloria's turn to check up on Grandma.

Somehow, as happens in certain close families, feathers got ruffled over the years. Siblings felt slighted at different points in the generations and stopped talking for stretches of time. Sons or daughters pulled away from parents. Relatives took sides. Trivial offenses rankled and became persistent frustrations. And since most still lived very near each other their insecurities and rivalries seemed to come out in full force when Grandma visited from California. She steered clear of the fray. When her first parent died she decided she wasn't going home for funerals, not her parents, not her siblings. What she did with the first would set a precedent, and if she couldn't maintain it, it would cause too much dissension. She mourned from afar. They kept track of the finest details of her stays: number of minutes and meals with each family. They looked for ways to gain a time advantage at the expense of one another. And they didn't limit it to Grandma. Two brothers—grown men—got in a shoving match over who was taking Mom to church when she was sixteen and visiting on her own.

But Grandma loved them all. As we reminded her about Gloria and Glen's call, she got choked up talking about her family. She wanted it to be known she always loved each and every one of them, even when they couldn't seem to get along with one another. And she tried her best to never show any partiality. I told her over and over each of them has always known how much she loved them, and each of them loved her, too. They adored her.

Her family's lack of a faith foundation must have bothered Grandma. She rarely talked about it, but today she brought up how she tried to work God into the letters she sent them. How she was never pushy, but she never let her faith fade into the background.

"Maybe this is the centerpiece . . . maybe they'll come together."

She was a little hard to follow as she tried to make it clear how very much she has prayed for her family over the years. How very much she wants them to know her Christ the way she does, not just in a Sunday kind of way, but in a life-changing kind of way. And she thinks they're getting closer. They talk about God now. It's a step. She won't let go of hope.

Mom headed home, and then Uncle Brian took Grandpa home. I had an hour and a half to myself with Grandma. She was tired. The pressure in her chest kept her hand fluttering and pressing at her breastbone. Not that she would call it that . . . "breast" is not in Grandma's vocabulary. She simply won't say it. We never ate chicken breasts at her house. We ate chicken chests.

She pulled me out of my reverie, *"Before I go, is there anything else you need to know?"*

How did she do that? How did she sweep my emotional feet right out from under me? One question and I was fighting tears.

"Everything. I need to know everything."

"We probably should have started this years ago."

"Oh, Grandma, we did. I think you've told me all these stories . . . I just love hearing them again. And, you know, you had a big family. I wasn't very good at keeping everyone straight when I was younger."

"I'm glad we had this time to talk."

"Me, too. Me, too. Talking to you is my favorite thing."

"You're sweet . . . are you going to stay with me?"

"Oh. No. Remember, I came straight here from work, and I'm going to go straight to Bible Study. But Grandpa will be here tomorrow morning. And as soon as Mom and I finish working, we'll be here, too."

"*That's right.*" Picking at the blankets. "*You have to work.*"

"I do. But I'll be here tomorrow. You can't shake me that easily. I just keep coming back."

"*Yes, you do.*"

"Grandma, do you know how much I love you?"

"*Let me see . . . all the rice in China?*"

"Even more. I was going to say to the moon and back, but I love you more than that. To the sun and back. I love you to the sun and back . . . and then a little more."

"*Okay. That's good.*"

"I love you, Grandma."

"*I love you, Honey.*"

Thursday, January 23

They were supposed to move Grandma today. But no one called to give me a new room number, so I called Mom for more information as I arrived at the hospital after work. The update on her scheduled release was getting more and more confusing and sounding less and less ideal. She was a categorical anomaly: not sick enough for the hospital or hospice, not likely enough to make progress in skilled nursing or rehab, not healthy enough for assisted living or in-home care. Mom met me with a hug inside the door to Grandma's unit as the hospitalist, Dr. Lee, walked up to us. He ran through the whole thing with us again. The new plan was to send her to rehab—without too much rehab—for a week or two as a way to "buy time" to see if she might shift into a category. The discussion left my emotions right on the tipping point of contained and uncontained.

Grandma woke up when she heard our voices greeting Grandpa. But she wouldn't open her eyes until I asked to see them. Then she locked eyes with me, and she was up.

There were a lot of tears. Mostly quiet tears. We tried to keep them out of her sight, but it was hard. They kept leaking out.

Mom stood by Grandma's bed, playing with her beautiful white hair. Leaning over to kiss her forehead she asked, "Mom, is there anything I can do for you?"

"No . . . . . . just pray for me."

Mom turned her head as she wept and struggled to find her voice. She whispered back, "I do."

I think I'm beginning to understand crying out to God. I'm not much of a crier. And I'm an internal processor—by the time words come out, they've been carefully chosen. But as I drove home from the hospital Thursday night I was crying, and when I could gather enough breath and control to get words out I spilled the scattered thoughts and emotions into the safe hands of Jesus. I cried out how scared I was of losing Grandma but how I would much rather lose her than have her suffer. I begged God to not allow Grandma to ever feel alone or scared but to be fully aware of His presence with her all through the night.

It makes me think of how less than a year ago I first allowed myself to start processing that I'd lose her someday, and I was already losing pieces of her as she lost pieces of herself.

I had hoped if Grandma had to have dementia, she wouldn't know. To know you don't know . . . is brutal.

But she knows.

She knows she's forgetting. She knows she's confused.

And I think for the very first time my heart is broken. Not a clean break. Countless, jagged fractures that just keep spreading.

I want so badly to wrap my arms around her and promise her it'll be okay.

Oh, if I could "fix" her. Even if fixing meant she forgot everything, but she didn't have to be aware of it. Or just to take away that horrible, terrible part of awareness that makes her embarrassed.

It's wrong. It's wrong for someone who has lived such an amazing life, who has loved so well and loved so many, who has courageously faced good and bad and hard so gracefully—it's wrong for her to be embarrassed about her mind's cruel frailty.

Because those who love her—which is everyone who has ever met her—will never be embarrassed. We will cry bitter tears, but our love for her and our pride in being her family can never be diminished.

I've never known a woman called mom, aunt or grandma by more people who aren't related to her than she is.

No matter what slips away, she will be the one who taught me to laugh, to love, to play kickball, to clean my plate, to respect stories as the currency of life.

Seeing the most resilient woman I know lose her place in her day takes my breath away. And it would be okay if we saw it and she didn't.

But she knows.

She knows she's forgetting. She knows she's confused.

And she can't remember that we don't care, that we will love her no matter what she forgets . . . even if it's us.

Friday, January 24

As I laid out my clothes, I thought I was being practical. Jeans for a Friday, but not too casual. A dressy-ish top and heels. The heels are less about the outfit and more about visiting Grandma since she loves the sound of heels. But this morning as I went to put on the necklace I wear with this top—it's the only one that works—I realized it's the pearl Grandma and Grandpa gave me when I graduated from high school. Even when I think I'm not thinking about Grandma, I'm thinking about Grandma.

The emotions of grief feel a lot like the remnants of crying: leaky, puffy, thick, achy, stinging, slow, dulled, in a tunnel. It feels so obvious from the inside—as though everyone looking at me can tell from a mile away—and yet life keeps going, and it isn't always apparent to the rest of the world that engaging with them means dropping the pieces of my heart I'm precariously holding in my hands.

Saturday, January 25—in the rehab place

I walked in right after the physical therapist, Jana. Assessment day. Grandpa, Dad and Mom left the room, while I stayed to help.

Jana had Grandma swing her legs to the left side of the bed and push herself up to a sitting position, legs dangling over the edge. Jana tested her leg strength, and then had Grandma scoot herself forward inch by inch until her feet touched the floor.

Kneeling in front of her Jana asked, "Maxine, do you know what year it is?"

"Two thousand . . . two thousand . . . I'm afraid I've lost it."

"That's okay. It's 2014."

"Oh . . . 2014."

"Do you know what month it is?"

Silence.

"We just had Christmas and then New Years, so it's . . ."

"January."

"Yes—January 2014."

With one hand holding onto the walker and one hand pushing off the bed, Grandma was up.

"I think I have to go potty," Grandma said with a look of surprise.

Jana pointed through the bathroom door to the toilet about 20 feet away. "Okay, it's right there."

"I don't know if I can make it."

"Let's try," Jana countered.

With a speed and determination I hadn't seen in ages, Grandma was off. She took the most direct route cutting tight corners and expertly navigating the walker. Her first time to get into a bathroom in weeks.

"Look at you go, Grandma! You're a pro."

The trip back to the bed was a bit slower, but no wasted movement. At the foot of the bed, Grandma's right hand let go of the walker.

"Are you okay?"

"I just thought I might tumble."

"You've got your walker, and Jana has you. You won't tumble."

"Okay."

"One step at a time."

Grabbing the walker she asked, *"Do I need to back in there?"*

Jana replied, "Yep, turn around . . . good. Slide to your left. A little more. A little more. This bed is a little high for you. Go ahead and sit down, and then I'll help with your legs."

"Grandma, you did amazing! Did you see how far you walked? Did that feel good?"

"*I'm tired!*"

Jana gently cradled Grandma as she lifted her legs up onto the bed. Grandma looked up at me.

"Don't get too comfy Grandma, you're way down at the bottom of the bed."

"*Should I scoot?*"

"Do you think you can scoot up that far?" Jana asked.

"*I'll try.*"

She centered herself in the bed but scooting up to the head of the bed was a bit much. So I moved around to the right side of the bed, and on the count of three Jana and I lifted Grandma up to the head of the bed.

"Grandma, you did such a good job! I had no idea you could walk that far . . . I think you've been holding out on us," I said with a grin.

"*Well you're such an encourager.*"

"You did great! And lunch should be here soon, you can just rest until then."

"*Okay.*"

Everyone else came back in and got the full report on Grandma's therapy, and then the lunch tray arrived.

"Okay, looks like we have a chicken and rice dish. And some green beans . . . I don't know what that is . . . chocolate Ensure, oh, and chocolate ice cream!" I said.

"Oh, Mom, you love chocolate ice cream!" Mom added.

"*I do.*"

"Want to start with it?"

"Kristen! Try for something healthy, please."

I whispered, "I tried, Grandma."

"*Yes, you did.*"

"I had Kookie Brittle for breakfast."

"*You did? Good for you.*"

Mom rolled her eyes, "You two. She gets it from you, Mom."

Grandma smiled at me.

After a few bites of the chicken and rice and a bite of beans, we started in on the ice cream with gusto.

Mom scanned the menu and said, "It says this is some kind of pureed wheat roll."

We exchanged raised eyebrows over the bed.

"Mom, do you want to try it?"

"*You try it.*"

I grinned as I gave Grandma another bite of ice cream. Mom took a bite of the "roll." And then I bit my lip as her face contorted. There was no more mention of Grandma trying the roll, but she did get down the entire bowl of ice cream.

Sunday, January 26

Lunch wasn't a big hit. After a few bites of the pork with peach sauce, one bite of cauliflower and a bite of mashed potatoes all washed down with chocolate Ensure, we moved on to the chocolate ice cream.

"Grandma, did you have ice cream on the farm?"

"*Oh, yes. One time Mom let me invite Floretta and Leta Mae. My brothers came home with their friends. Uncle Pete and Uncle Gene were there. And Mom invited some Conklin couples. We had five gallons of ice cream. You had to eat it right away. We couldn't keep it.*"

"Because you couldn't keep it frozen?"

"*Right, there was no way to keep it that cold.*"

"Did you get to eat as much as you wanted?"

"*Oh, yes!*"

"I bet you loved that."

"*I thought I was really living.*"

"What was your favorite thing your mom made?"

"*Bread.*"

"Bread?"

"*She made her own bread. Every Saturday she'd bake bread.*"

"Did that last the whole week?"

"*No . . . maybe she made it another day, too. We ate it so fast.*"

"Did you help in the kitchen?"

"Not really. Mom was such a good cook. Sometimes I'd make a cake or something."

"What about on your birthday? What did she make then?"

"Oh, you know! She'd make fudge cake or maybe a yellow cake."

"Did she only make fudge cake for special occasions?"

"Yes . . . you make fudge cake."

"A few times. Grandma Borgman's Fudge Cake is what I picture when I picture a birthday cake."

"You know we didn't really get presents or things. There just wasn't that kind of money. But one year Mom said I could invite Floretta and Leta Mae over. She was fixing supper and I saw Leta Mae coming through her father's fields and Floretta coming up the road. And she was carrying a package. I was so excited. It was wrapped in newspaper. When I got to open it I just couldn't believe how lucky I was to have a present. I unwrapped it, and it was newspaper inside."

"Newspaper wrapped in newspaper?"

"Yes."

"Were you disappointed?"

"Probably a little disappointed. But I got to unwrap a present."

. . .

"Boy, this hurts. I've never felt anything like this in my life. I don't know how to explain it."

"I'm sorry. I wish I could make it hurt less . . . Once the medicine absorbs, it should stop hurting."

"I don't mean to be a baby."

"You aren't a baby! You're the strongest person I know."

"Wowzers! It's like hot scissors slicing through the skin."

"Oh, Grandma, I'm sorry! I can get you some more ice . . . It should stop hurting in a couple hours. Is there anything I can do to help you feel better?"

"Just pray. Pray I won't be a baby."

"You aren't a baby! Let's pray now."

"Okay."

Stroking her hand I prayed, "Dear Jesus, we ask that you would take this pain away from Grandma. Please help the medicine to do its job without hurting her. And when it does hurt, we ask that you would give her the strength to get through it and know that you are right here with her every minute. Help her to be brave and keep fighting. And remind her that you love her even more than we do— I don't know how that's possible because we love her so much, but we know it's true—you love her even more. Thank you that she's feeling better and getting stronger. We love you. In Jesus' name, amen."

With tears in her eyes, "*I don't think I'm very brave.*"

"You are! You're the bravest person I know, Grandma. And you never complain."

"*I think I just did.*"

In the rehab place it's hard for me to get a chair close enough to Grandma's bed to hear her and really talk, so I sit on the edge of her bed. I'd been sitting there holding her hand for over an hour when she finally fell asleep. Her fluid-filled right forearm—where the IV had failed—was resting on a surgical glove filled with ice. I was sitting on her left side but reaching across her body to hold her right hand. When she fell asleep, it occurred to me I was sitting in an awkward position. Before long my left foot fell asleep and my back started to ache from the way it was twisted. But there was no way I could wake Grandma up to reposition myself.

An hour into her nap, her eyes opened wide. She jerked her hand out of mine and pulled her right arm up to her chest.

"*It's cold.*"

"Your arm has been on ice."

"*I'm cold.*"

As I wrapped her shoulder cozy more tightly around her to cover any exposed skin I asked, "How's your arm?"

"*It's fine. I'm cold.*"

"But your arm feels better?"

"*Yes. It's cold.*"

"Okay, let me move the ice."

I grabbed the glove of ice. Walking around her bed to put it on the tray I stretched my back and rolled my shoulders. I turned around to tell her how glad I was her arm was feeling better, but she was sound asleep.

Wednesday, January 29

I hadn't seen Grandma for two days. She was asleep when Mom and I walked in, but she started coughing. I saw her eyes flicker open. "Grandma, do you need a tissue?" If anything would get her attention it would be a tissue. My whole life she's always had a tissue in her hand or her pocket. In the hospital she went through boxes and boxes of the cheap, one-ply tissues. We couldn't keep her in tissue. Nurses brought in several boxes at a time. Now in the rehab place she has real, soft two-ply tissues, but she doesn't seem to need them quite as much.

As I offered the tissue her eyes searched my face.

"*Oh, hi, Honey.*"

I fixed her covers then took my seat on the edge of her bed holding her hand.

"*Did you have a good day today?*"

"It was fine. Just long. Lots of meetings and things. But now I'm here, so it's great."

"*You're so sweet.*"

"Do you know what story I was thinking about today?"

"*What?*"

"Remember when you had a friend over to spend the night, and it was winter, and you didn't want to go out to the outhouse, so you found a hatbox?"

"*Oh, yes!*"

"Will you tell me that one again?"

"*Floretta was spending the night, and we'd gotten undressed and into our pajamas. Then we realized we'd forgotten to go to the outhouse. But it was so cold. I thought we could use that hatbox, so we tinkled in it.*"

"Was it Aunt Dollie's?"

"*I think so. The next day my aunt and uncle were over, and Dad saw a spot on the ceiling in the parlor. He said, 'Emma, I think we have a leak.'*"

"*That was no leak!*"

"Did you tell your dad?"

"*Not for a few years.*"

"How old were you?"

"*Oh, we were teenagers.*"

"I thought you were a little girl!"

As Mom and I sat on either side of Grandma holding her hands we laughed and talked about each of our Michigan memories. Grandma and I talked about my high school graduation trip with her to meet the family and see the places: whom we stayed with, where we went, what we ate.

"Do you remember how excited I was about all the trees and how green everything was? I'm pretty sure they all thought I was a nut. I'd just never seen trees like that! Or open space between towns. Remember when we were driving from Aunt Dollie's out to Jim's house in Fruitport and I couldn't believe there was 'country' in between?"

Chuckling and smiling, *"Yes."*

"What was your favorite part about that trip?"

"Oh, just about everything."

I remember riding with Marlene and Gordon one afternoon. I think we'd just been out to McNitt Cemetery to visit Grandma and Grandpa Borgman's graves and Bernice and Byron's. We were going for ice cream, and Gordon commented on the skunk smell. The two of them were gagging in the front seat while Grandma practically had her head hanging out the window. I knew she loved the smell of skunk, but I had never smelled one before—that was the moment I found out I loved it, too. I'm my grandmother's granddaughter.

When the conversation slowed, Grandma looked off between us. "Whatcha thinking, Grandma?"

"I was just thinking I wish I had my life to live over."

"What would you do differently, Mom?"

"Probably nothing . . . All this reminiscing just makes me homesick."

"There're lots of good memories, aren't there?" Mom asked, "More good than bad."

"Yes."

There's a melancholy today I hadn't seen before. It's not the dementia or the discomfort of being ill. It's an exhaustion deep in her bones. An intense desire to be done. And a level of emotion, a sentimentality, rarely displayed. Each goodbye—to Grandpa, to Mom, to me—tearier than the last. Each memory harder to leave behind, a present harder to engage with and a future beyond focus.

She's so ready to go. As she told the doctor yesterday, *"I just want to be comfortable until I can go be with my Lord."*

It makes it both easier and harder to wrestle with the emotions and thoughts as they wash over me. I think about what I wrote a few months ago:

"So many things feel like lasts . . ."

The tears slid down my cheeks and the rest of the words stuck sideways in my throat. Another syllable would bring uncontrollable sobbing.

The silence screamed: *did I say that?* Did I verbally admit I think every time I'm with my grandma—every birthday, every card game, every conversation, every meal, every holiday, every hug—could be the last?

I choked out, "We need to talk about something happy now."

My friend offered the silence and space she knew I needed, but I begged off, "I don't want to think about this right now."

She paused. Then she carried the conversation to its end. She tried to distract me from the undistractable—I don't want to think about it . . . but I can't stop.

My grandma is *that* person. She's the person I want to be like, the person who shapes so many memories, the person whose stories I grew up on. The thought of ever saying goodbye is the most unthinkable thought I've tried to think.

And part of why it's so hard is because she's the person I always wanted to share important life moments with, moments I haven't had yet. I wanted her to be at my wedding. I wanted her to hold my children and tell them stories. I wanted her to read my first book—a book I always assumed would be about her.

But I'm 33 and she's 89. And she's ready to go home. After decades of defying her age it's mounted an offense she doesn't have the strength to fight.

And the truth is, I'm not just grieving that she won't be part of all those life moments. I'm grieving that I probably won't have most of them. And I won't have them without her. How can I face losing my dreams without my grandma? I'm a teary, mucus-y, gasping mess at the possibility.

Somehow I thought as long as she was here, those other things would fall into place. But it's getting harder to ignore our realities.

I'd give every last dream to have her. I can imagine life without dreams. I cannot imagine life without her, and it seems cruel that I have to.

Saturday, February 1

Grandma had a lot of physical therapy this morning. Despite many failed attempts at learning to ride a bike over the years—one of her biggest regrets—the therapist attached a wheel/pedal attachment to her wheelchair today and she "rode a bike," and then she walked fifty steps. She hit the high end of her daily goal.

But it tired her out, and she'd been asleep almost an hour and a half when we arrived.

She woke up a few minutes later.

"You can sleep longer, Grandma."

"I don't want to sleep while you're here."

"Do you know how lucky I am to be your granddaughter? I'm more than lucky. I'm blessed."

"You're so special. Such a sweetheart."

"Remember how you used to call us 'creature' and 'cuteheart'?"

"Yes."

"Where did that come from?"

"Oh, I don't know."

"Well, you can call me 'creature' or 'cuteheart' any time."

As we worked on getting a few bites of lunch down, Uncle Brian and Aunt Jill arrived. It was a party in Grandma's room.

"Grandma, when you used to get a stick of gum, was it Floretta you shared it with?"

"Floretta and Leta Mae."

"You took turns, right?"

"Yes."

"How long would you keep it?"

"As long as I could—sometimes weeks—until Mother would find it."

"What do you mean?" Uncle Brian asked.

"At night I'd stick it to my bedpost, and sometimes it would get really stuck. It'd pull a little varnish off with it. But I didn't care. I'd keep chewing it. We'd take turns, trading days. Until my mom would find it on the bedpost and then she'd throw it out."

"That's disgusting!" Uncle Brian said.

Grandpa chimed in, "Tell him what else you'd chew."

"Tar."

"That was in the summer when the road got hot, right?" I asked.

"Yes. We'd pull some up and ball it up and then chew it."

"I can't imagine that tasted good."

"I'm sure it didn't."

"You loved gum, didn't you, Mom?" Mom asked. "Wasn't the joke they couldn't tell if you chewed faster or typed faster?"

"Oh, yes. One day my boss walked up behind me while I was typing and said, 'Maxine, what would happen if you stopped chewing gum?'

"And I said, 'I think I'd have to give up my career.'"

Then more visitors arrived. Marge and Carol Clark and Jeannien Swift came in with freshly cut roses and a cow card. The Clarks and Grandma have exchanged cow-themed gifts for years, and it brought an immediate smile to Grandma's face.

The roses went next to the camellias the Hills brought yesterday.

Each day Grandpa brings in the cards that arrive for Grandma. Cards come in from all over for the woman who maintained decades of correspondence with people across the country. Some were old friends, some were people she only met once on an airplane but stayed in touch with nonetheless.

When I was little it seemed Grandma was always one of two places when I got to their house: in the kitchen or at her Electrolux typewriter. I loved to watch her fingers fly over the keys. And if she wasn't typing a letter, she was writing a card. I learned from Grandma about matching the pen ink to the color of the type in a card. I can still picture her colorful collection of Marvy Le Pen and Pilot Rollerball pens—I dreamed of the day I'd be old enough to have grown-up, colored pens like Grandma did. But my favorite letters I got at summer camp came from her typewriter. Her chatty, funny, anecdote-heavy missives. She never adjusted to the word processor. And by the time email invaded, she gave up the keyboard and dictated to Grandpa instead. She still sent cards, but it was never quite the same as the typewriter.

I remember getting to their house one day, and Grandma was wrapping a present on the kitchen table. It was for my birthday. As I looked at the odd shape of the package, I realized it looked just like the shape of her typewriter. I was no more than five or six, so I should have been happy a few days later when I unwrapped a Cabbage Patch doll instead, but a little part of me was sad I didn't get a typewriter like Grandma's.

Now we read her cards to her, and we give the update on phone calls. Her nieces and nephews in Michigan call. And friends in Colorado, Illinois, Texas, Arizona, Nevada and all over California want constant updates. Meeting Grandma is knowing Grandma. Knowing Grandma is loving Grandma. I've never met anyone as loved as she is.

Monday, February 2

I find myself flossing each tooth with the utmost care and brushing for the full two minutes and even using mouthwash for one piece of lettuce stuck between two teeth. Why? Because I can. Because I can control the cleanliness of my teeth. I can't control how Grandma feels or what she remembers or how many breaths she has left, but I can control my dental hygiene. In my helplessness I can do this.

While doctors debate if progressing means progress and try to calculate number of days and how that fits into a clinical care formula, I am useless. I can do nothing. I want to scream—there is a soul inside that body. We are not discussing data. We are discussing life.

A life I love more than words can express.

I understand plans need to be made. I understand there are forms and hoops and insurance conundrums. I do. I really do. But I don't care. I have one plan. Love my grandma.

I can't worry about the number of days or the classification of her care. There isn't enough room in my brain. I'm too busy memorizing every inch of her face, the feel of her hand in mine, the sound of her voice, the curve of her smile, the look in her eye as the decades melt away and she's a girl on a farm in Michigan again. I need the space to remember how my name sounds slipping through her lips when I walk into the room and how precisely and intently she shapes the words, "I love you" before I leave.

I need every bit of mental and emotional capacity to help her find her place in an increasingly unfamiliar world. When she says she can't remember what home looks like, I need to be able to help her conjure the people she loves more than places, so she has somewhere to feel safe in the midst of another nondescript medical facility. I need every last reserve to be able to hold her hands and pray her well being out of our hands and into Jesus'.

I'm not sure what form I was expecting grief to arrive in, but it wasn't this. It wasn't an ability to accept a lack of control but not an ability to accept a lack of compassion. I am not angry she is dying. I am angry she is living through precious waking moments without hearing how loved she is. I am angry people have the audacity to waste her time discussing her physical prognosis instead of discussing how deeply she has influenced their lives. I am angry anyone cares what she is forgetting when what she remembers is so much more important. I am angry we are wasting words when there is so much left to be said and to be heard. And where she is matters little as long as we are with her. Not physically in the same room, but *with* her, fully present.

Because I don't think the day will come when I will wish I had spent more time understanding the delineations between rehab and skilled nursing and hospice. But I know I will wish I had spent more time reveling in her stories.

So I tell her I love her—over and over and over—because I can. I hold her hand. I stare into her eyes. I put ChapStick on her dry lips. I ask for the stories I know by heart. I wander the bumpy rabbit trails of her memory. I dig for the details I might not have time to ask about later. I stay longer than I mean to, and I count the minutes until I can come back again. Because I can. And someday I won't be able to; but today, today I can.

What I can do—whether caring for my grandma or my teeth—I will do as well as I possibly can. Because I can.

Wednesday, February 5

Today was the day. Hospice.

I can't quite wrap my head around it. Or maybe it's my heart that refuses to bend.

Another move. I didn't understand how disorienting moves are when dementia throws so many other wrenches into staying oriented. But Grandma handled it with her usual grace. It's not the home she thought she was going to—and there were definitely some blank looks behind her smiles as people came to greet her and welcome her "back" to her new home in the skilled nursing wing—but at least now she's only a few long halls away from Grandpa and their apartment . . . even if she doesn't know it and can't navigate the way.

When Mom left to walk Grandpa back to the apartment, she reached for my hand, *"Kristen . . . I'm glad we have a . . . special relationship. You're a fun niece."*

"We do have a special relationship, don't we? I'm so lucky to be your granddaughter. I don't think any of my friends have had as much fun with their grandmas. We've made a lot of fun memories."

"We have . . . I know you have more important places to be—"

"*This* is my more important place to be. Being with you is my important place."

"Oh . . . you're so special."

A soft knock at the door interrupted us.

"Even the chef visits! Grandma, Jeff is here."

I could tell from her smile she knew she should know him, but she was struggling to place his face. He knelt next to her bed and held her hand. "I heard a rumor you were back. There's no admitting paperwork, so I don't know what I get to make for you—what sounds good?"

"*Oh* . . ."

"You haven't had much appetite have you? But maybe now Jeff will be able to find something you like."

"Are we doing nectars?" Jeff asked.

Grandma looked back and forth between us, so holding her gaze I said, "Well, you don't like the thickened water, do you? But it has been a pureed diet."

"So some swallowing trouble?" Jeff asked.

"Not really. You did fine with the swallowing tests. It just takes a very long time for you to chew food, and it's been tiring you out, hasn't it? They were hoping you'd eat a little more and get some more calories in you when they switched you from finely chopped to pureed."

Laughing and looking at me, Jeff said, "You're learning all the lingo!"

"It's been an educational few weeks . . . But ice cream is always a favorite. That's one thing you always eat."

"We can do ice cream. And milk shakes. I can do milk shakes to get some other things in . . . We'd like you to eat more than just ice cream." Jeff said while rubbing the back of her hand.

"*I don't think I'm a very good pet.*"

"You don't think you're a very good bet?"

"*A very good pet.*"

Shooting his eyebrows up, Jeff said, "Well I think you'd be a good pet. I don't think you'd dig up my yard like my dog does. Do you dig holes?"

"*I could try.*"

"And here I was being so nice. I didn't even short-sheet your bed!"

"Oh, Grandma, Jeff knows your tricks!"

"The world needs practical jokers," Jeff added.

Later more visitors arrived as Mom and I got ready to leave. The lost look returned to Grandma's eyes, but she listened to their happy greetings.

I leaned in to say goodbye. "Okay, I'll see you tomorrow."

"Okay, Honey."

"I love you, I love you, I love you."

"Oh, I love you."

I glanced back from the doorway to see a look of gracious bewilderment as she tried to find the right responses for the faces swimming at the end of her bed talking about a room she'd never seen before being home. And not a word of complaint or disagreement as she thanked the seeming strangers for coming to see her.

Thursday, February 6

The sound of my heels on the hardwood floor caused Grandma to stir. I saw her hand fidget with the blanket.

"Hi, Grandma," I whispered.

Her head turned and one eye opened. As I came into view she opened both eyes and smiled, *"Oh, hi, Honey."*

"Are you cold?"

"No, I'm okay." She reached for her right shoulder and winced.

"Are you okay? Is your arm bothering you?"

"My shoulder hurts."

"Would you like me to see if the nurse could give you some Tylenol?"

"That might be good."

"Okay . . . did you want to sit up a bit?"

"That might be nice."

"Hold on, this might be a wild ride."

She raised both arms and clenched her fists. No loss of humor here. This is the woman who decided in her seventies to ride the roller coaster at Mall of America for the thrill—of course she's also the woman who didn't tell anyone about the pain it caused in her eye, which ultimately turned out to be an acute narrow angle glaucoma attack that permanently damaged her vision. Once the head of her bed was raised she looked me full in the face.

"You have such nice skin."

"Oh, Grandma, I think your vision is going! You're the one with good skin. I wish I'd gotten your skin. Somehow that didn't trickle down."

"I used to pray for a nice complexion."

"Well it worked or you're a late bloomer because your skin is beautiful."

"That must be it. I was a late bloomer . . . I'm so glad you're my granddaughter."

"And I'm so glad you're my grandma."

Barbara from Activities came in to do a questionnaire. She asked grandma questions about where she was born, her husband, her education level and then she asked what her career had been. One word: secretary.

Snippets of stories washed over me as Barbara notated secretary. I thought of Grandma in the defense plant and at Birds Eye Frozen Foods where she became lifelong friends with Rosemary and met Mom's dad and later at Magnolia where she perfected her jokes with Gladys and then at Biola where she introduced a level of levity I'm sure the history department is still recovering from almost thirty years later. It was as a part-time secretary for the history professors that Grandma began baking her cookies full of cayenne pepper and other replacement ingredients. And as professors would cough and gag, she'd lift the candy bowl from her desk and offer them a chocolate to get the flavor out of their mouths. Why they'd eat anything else she offered them never made sense, but every time they'd take one of her candies—chocolate-covered Ivory soap, hand-dipped.

Of course, she didn't limit her food gags to her bosses. My brothers and I ate our fair share of non-desserts. I'm the only one who swallowed the chocolate-covered soap—I didn't know what else to do once it was in my mouth. But on April Fools' Day we fell for her freshly baked "treats" year after year. In seventh grade I kept chewing and chewing the cookie that wouldn't break down in my mouth. I was gagging as I ran to a trash can to spit it out. When I looked up, I saw my brother across the quad doubled-over a can spitting out his own cotton ball-laced cookie. Eventually we learned the only safe April Fools' was if it fell on Sunday—even Grandma had her standards.

When the nurse came in, Barbara said she'd come back a different time to finish the questionnaire, and she slipped out. After Grandma took the Tylenol, the nurse slid the mask on her for a breathing treatment. Grandma's never been a fan of them, but this time the sound was different—not rhythmic at all. This struck Grandma as funny, and she started giggling. Then she began pinching the tube and mask to further alter the sounds, which only made her laugh more. But the noise of her oxygen and the breathing treatment was too much for her weak voice to talk over, and within a few minutes she fell asleep.

When her breathing treatment finished, I turned the machine off and carefully slipped the mask off, so as not to disturb her. She woke a few minutes later.

"You can keep resting, Grandma."

"I think maybe I will."

"Okay . . . I'm going to go ahead and go. You rest, and I'll see you tomorrow."

"Oh, no! Stay a little longer."

"Okay. Go to sleep, I'll be right here."

She reached out a shaky hand to hold mine. Apparently there is something about that "grand" relationship. Just as my mom can't say no to her grandchildren, I can't say no to my grandma. As she fell asleep the shaking stopped, her hand relaxed and yet somehow tightened its grip on mine. For twenty-two minutes I held her hand and watched her sleep . . . and prayed.

When she woke again I tucked her in snugly and kissed her goodbye.

"I love you so much."

"I love you so very much. I'll be back tomorrow."

Friday, February 7

As I walked through the door I could see Grandma shaking in

her bed. It's the shake she does when she's nauseated—a full-body shudder and grimace.

"Hi Grandma, how are you feeling?"

"*Oh, Honey . . . sick.*"

"Should I call the nurse?"

"*I think someone did.*"

After stepping into the hall and verifying the nurse was coming with anti-nausea medicine, I knelt next to Grandma's bed.

"*I think I might upchuck.*"

"That's okay. Let's sit up a little more. If you need to, go ahead," I said as I held a grey plastic, five-quart rectangular "bowl" under her chin.

A nurse walked in as I rubbed Grandma's back and held the bowl for her and she vomited the small bit of bile in her system. I wiped her nose and helped her rinse her mouth as another nurse walked in with a crushed up anti-nausea pill mixed with applesauce.

"Grandma, I know it doesn't sound good, but if you could take just a bite or two of this, it should help calm your tummy . . . do you think you can get it down?"

"*I'll try.*" Grandma shook and groaned, but down it went.

That's when the nurse mentioned Grandma was refusing to eat aside from her Ensure. Coupled with the narcotic pain medicine it was no wonder her stomach was upset.

"Narcotic pain medicine?"

"The Methadone."

"She's on Methadone?!? For what? She hasn't been in pain. She's had Tylenol twice when she was achy from being in bed."

The nurse shrugged. Then the mask went on for a breathing treatment.

I sat and rubbed her arm. And every time she asked how much longer I told her how brave she was and how close she was to being done. When I took the mask off, she said she might upchuck some more.

"You can if you need to, but it's only been about twenty minutes since you took the medicine that's supposed to help your stomach. It'd be great if you could keep that down so it could help you feel better."

"*Okay . . . you're a special granddaughter.*"

"You're a special grandma—I guess that makes us a special pair."

"*I think we are.*"

"Is there anything I can do to make you feel better?"

"*Maybe the ol' soft shoe?*"

"Well, then I'd be in bed next to you with a broken leg! I didn't do so hot in dance class when I was six."

"*Sing?*"

"Oh, that wouldn't be much better. I'm as bad as Mom. Maybe we should steer clear of things involving rhythm . . . I could read to you. Do you have a favorite Psalm?"

"*Oh, I can't think . . .*"

"How about Psalm 62? That's one Mom read to me when I was in the hospital after my appendectomy. Remember that? That was a long time ago now."

I lingered on Psalm 62:8, "Trust in him at all times, you people; pour out your hearts to him, for God is our refuge."

After I finished reading, Grandma nodded off. I held her hand and rubbed her arm. When she woke up, I asked, "How are you feeling?"

"*Pretty good.*"

"Let's lay you back a bit, so you can rest more comfortably . . . do you want me to stay awhile longer?"

"*You have things to do.*"

"I don't have anywhere to be. How about I stay a little longer? But if you fall asleep, is it okay if I leave while you're sleeping?"

"*I think so.*"

I held her hand until she was soundly asleep, and then I tiptoed out so my heels wouldn't waken her.

Saturday, February 8

Grandma was sitting up in a wheelchair when Mom and I walked in just before noon. She'd had a good morning but had started feeling nauseated shortly before we arrived.

Turns out Grandma was getting Methadone twice a day. Between calls from the nurse to hospice and from Aunt Jill to hospice, the Methadone was taken off and it was back to two Tylenol as needed. No more narcotics.

Visitors came and went. A couple—M.J. and Peter —from the independent living side, a former neighbor, a former employee of the retirement home, the Clarks, Dad, us. Grandma's popularity has not decreased.

Lunch was more successful than most meals: a dozen bites of food and half a can of Ensure. Practically a record.

As I kissed her goodbye I said I'd see her tomorrow.

"Promise?"

"I promise. I'll see you tomorrow."

Sunday, February 9

Tomorrow is Uncle Brian's fifty-first birthday. I stopped in after church to let Grandma know I'd be back later for the party. She was sitting up in her wheelchair but so tired. She wasn't sure how long she'd been up—the immediate details of the day are becoming more and more elusive.

As the nurse helped her back to bed for a pre-lunch nap, she said Grandma had been in the chair since breakfast, which would have been at least three hours. When she's sitting in the chair, she curves even farther forward and to the right than usual. She ends up staring at her lap and appears to be on the verge of tipping right out of the chair, though it doesn't seem to bother her at all.

When we arrived at 6:00 for the party Grandma was already in the day room at the head of the table sipping coffee. The woman who can't feed herself can still brush her own teeth and manage a cup and saucer full of hot coffee—I do believe we're being suckered. She looked tired. Grandpa kept bellowing at her that we were together to celebrate Brian's fifty-first birthday. She knew. Her hearing has never been an issue. She wished him a happy birthday.

It was quite the gathering. Both her children, four out of five grandchildren and one out of three great-grandchildren. And then Kevin pulled out his phone. For the very first time Grandma got to see her new, three-week old great-grandson live on FaceTime. He stared intently into the camera and right at Grandma as he worked his way through a bottle. Hopefully soon it can be an in-person meeting when he's gained enough weight to venture out of the house to more exciting places than the doctor's office.

Grandma's tummy wasn't feeling great, but she wanted to try the chocolate cake. I gave her the tiniest bite I could get on a fork, but it was a bit too rich and didn't stay down. She was not feeling well, but she's never been one to leave a party early.

To take her mind off her troubles Kev called Jon, and Grandma got to FaceTime with Jon, Angela and Norah. All the grandchildren (Jonathan [Angela], Kevin [Wendy], Kristen, Jessica, Amy) and great-grandchildren (Kayla, Norah, Aaron) in one night either in person or via video chat—not something she can lock into her memory, but something her heart never forgets.

Several employees who work in food services found reasons to pop in to see Grandma during the party. It was amazing to watch young women in their teens and early twenties kneel next to her and tell her how glad they were she was back and how much they'd missed her while she was gone. Daisy made sure to tell her they were the ones writing the notes on her meal tickets. With meals delivered to her room, they missed getting to talk to her in person like they used to in the dining hall. To say they adore her isn't strong enough.

Back in her room, as a nurse and I undressed Grandma to get her ready for bed I reminded her how very, very loved she is. It might have been a party for Uncle Brian, but people really wanted an excuse to be with her. Any opportunity to be with her was a good one in our book.

"You're a sweetie . . . you're so good to me."

"You're the most amazing woman I know!"

"I don't know about that."

"I do! And it's not just me. I've only been around for the last thirty-three years. But apparently you were quite amazing before I came along," I teased. "Everyone who's met you has a story and remembers you. You make quite an impression—you always have."

"Oh, you're sweet."

"I'm not sure if I'll be here tomorrow, but I'll be back soon, okay?"

"Okay, Honey."

"Good night. I love you, I love you, I love you."

"I love you . . . I love you . . . I love you . . . I love you . . . I love you . . . I love you."

Monday, February 10

Last night wasn't one of Grandma's best nights. Angela and Wendy—who hadn't been able to see Grandma since she got sick—were quite surprised at her appearance when they FaceTimed with her. But when Mom and I walked in after work today she was reclining in bed with one arm behind her head laughing and talking with Donna and her daughter, Lynn. She looked like a different woman.

"Grandma, look at you, all smiles!" I said as I gave Grandma a kiss. "It's almost unfair you can look this beautiful without even trying."

"I can't even remember the last time I looked in a mirror. It's been . . . I can't remember!"

"Well, you don't need one. You look great."

Donna said, "We're going to go. We'll free up these chairs for you."

"Oh, you don't need to go," Mom said, "Kristen's a bed-sitter."

"Yep, I am. I want to be as close as I can get."

Grandma grinned at me and chucked me under the chin as Donna and Lynn made their way out of the room with a promise to visit again soon.

Mom sat down by Grandma. "Hi Mom, you look beautiful."

"I must be sick."

"And you're funny," Mom added.

"I must be really sick."

Mom laughed. "How are you feeling today? Better than yesterday?"

"I think so."

We recounted the non-events of our workday. And then talk turned to the farm.

"Mom, tell Kristen about your R's. I don't think she knows that one."

"I don't!"

"Oh, yes! I didn't say my R's. When Dollie and I were planting in the garden I told her to put in the seed and I'd cov-uh it up. And everyone laughed. I knew they were laughing at me. So I kept doing it. I knew I'd get a laugh."

"What was it Verlyn would do?" Mom asked.

"It drove Verlyn crazy. She would kneel down in front of me and hold my shoulders and say, 'Say my name. Say Ver-lyn. I know you can do it.'

"And I'd say, 'Vuh-lyn.'

"Then she'd say, 'Mother, make her say it. She can say her R's. I know it.'

"And she was right, I could. I just didn't."

"How old were you? Like five?"

"Oh no, you were older weren't you?" Mom asked.

"I was," Grandma laughed. *"A few years older probably."*

"I know Verlyn was a hard worker, like with housework, but wasn't she the one who didn't really want to work in the fields? Maybe thought it was beneath her?" Mom asked.

"She didn't like to get her hands dirty. Dollie and I thought it was so funny . . . and when her boyfriend Bill Koglin would come to take her back to Grand Rapids she'd be in the parlor—which was for special guests and occasions, we didn't use it much—primping. Oh, I would just imitate her, I thought it was so funny."

Aunt Verlyn spent less time on the farm. As the oldest girl, she was only a few years from starting work when the family moved from Oregon back to Michigan to save the farm. Dollie, Bernice and Grandma only knew farm life since they were born there, but Verlyn and Sally weren't farm girls at heart.

When it was time to go, I told Grandma I wasn't sure if I'd see her tomorrow or if it would be Wednesday, but that I'd be back as soon as I could. Grandma let her smile melt away and her chin started to quiver. I laughed as I cupped her chin in my hand, "Oh, you can't keep me away for long! You know that."

She grinned.

"I love you, I love you, I love you."

"I love you . . . I love you . . . I love you . . . I love you . . . I love you . . . I love you . . . I can't say it as fast as you."

"Well, it's not a race."

"Oh good. Then I win."

Wednesday, February 12

Mom and I went straight from work to visit Grandma. Almost 48 hours without seeing her and I was getting antsy. She was sound asleep when we walked in, so Mom asked the nurse how long Grandma had been sleeping. The nurse said at least an hour and a half but that she was getting ready to give her some medicine. After we double-checked which medications Grandma was getting, we went in to wait for the nurse to wake Grandma—no reason for us to be the bad guys.

Grandma was all smiles when she saw us, and though the mask for a breathing treatment went right on she tried to talk over the noise.

Mom said something, and Grandma responded with, *"You got everything from your dad."*

In a split second Mom tried to discern if Grandma really meant her biological father or the dad who stepped in and chose her fifty-two years ago. Unsure if it was an attempted compliment or a slight dig, Mom asked, "Even how to bake a pie?"

"Well, he was half-baked."

Biological father.

Grandma's always been open about Mom's father. She would answer any question and made sure to tell good stories about him and show us pictures of him. That wasn't the most talked-about period of her life, but it was not ignored. Grandma met Joseph Gutweiler, a man almost fifteen years her senior, when she was a secretary at Birds Eye, a division of General Foods. The handsome, successful salesman's social drinking would ultimately turn into all-consuming alcoholism. And after he'd moved his family from California to Georgia and then lost his job a year later, he was given a choice: Maxine and Joanne or alcohol. He chose alcohol.

Grandma chose to return to California so she and Mom could start life over near friends. They drove across the country—with Joe, who also wanted to return to Los Angeles, passed out in the backseat—singing all the way. Once back, Grandma became a single, working mother in the late 1950s. Love filled in where money was short.

But today was not a day she chose to dwell long in that era of the past, she slipped back farther to her childhood.

"One day I was on the porch, and the dogs were barking, so I knew someone was coming. I was so excited. We didn't get a lot of company on the farm. The dogs wouldn't stop. I didn't understand because we didn't cater to animals on the farm. And then someone told me, 'Maxine, this is your aunt, so-and-so, and your uncle.'"

Mom asked, "Had they come from a long way away?"

"Wisconsin."

"Oh, so on your Mom's side. Wait, are these the people who came and stayed and stayed?" Mom asked.

"Before. I don't remember it really, but I was told they showed up one day with everything on their backs."

"Was it just your aunt and uncle or a whole family?" I asked.

"An entire family. I don't know if they were hungry or what."

"They stayed for months didn't they?" Mom asked.

"Yes."

Later I asked, "Grandma, did Uncle Byron always live in Michigan?"

"I think so."

"But he didn't come home as often on weekends, did he?"

"Oh, no. Well, and he was studying at the Ferris Institute."

"Was that in Michigan?"

"Yes."

"Did you ever get to go visit him there?"

"Yes. He always prided himself on not liking children, but he was happy to take me around. I think John took Mom and me to visit Byron."

"You were his favorite!" Mom said.

"I think I was. One weekend he was home, and he was in the parlor, and he said, 'Sis, come here. Come here, Sis.'

"So I went over, he was kind of crouched down, and he shielded me with his

body. He was listening in because Dollie and Mom were going at it."

"Aunt Dollie got sassy, didn't she?" Mom asked.

"Oh, she did! Mom asked her to stir whatever was on the stove, and she said, 'I will if I get to it.' That was a negative.

"And Byron could not understand. He believed if you earned a demerit, you had it coming. He did not understand Dollie sassing."

"The rest of you didn't sass did you?"

"No. She covered all of us."

As usual, I was sitting on the bed holding Grandma's hand. She reached over and began to scratch my hand.

"Do I have an itch?"

"One of us does."

I moved my hand so Grandma could scratch her own hand. She finished and then re-gripped mine.

"Do you feel better?"

"I do."

Mom laughed, "Oh, you two."

"You know I might be a little bit hungry."

"That's great!"

For the first time in over a month, Grandma was actually hungry. But when her dinner arrived, she didn't like it. She ate a few bites. Mom sampled each thing and agreed it was not the best. So Grandma settled in alternating between Ensure, coffee and vanilla ice cream.

Mom was not thrilled at how readily I let the real food go by the wayside and pushed the ice cream. As I offered another bite, she said, "And you think I don't say no to Kayla."

"Well, you want it to go the other way someday, don't you?" I answered.

I believe as the granddaughter it is my role to say no as infrequently as possible to my grandparents. If it is in my power to do what they want, I will do it. And if Grandma wants ice cream for dinner, that's fine by me. Besides, she was drinking her Ensure. The nurses keep saying as long as she does that they aren't concerned over what else she does or doesn't eat. That's all the license I need to indulge Grandma every chance I get.

When Grandpa got there he opened the two pink bags Max and

Salina Kennedy left when they visited this afternoon. The first bag had a box of Andes mints.

"Mom, do you want a mint?"

"I do."

Surprised, I grabbed the box and opened it for Grandma. She ate her mint in two bites and washed it down with coffee. No problem.

Meanwhile Grandpa opened the second bag and pulled out an assortment of Valentine's candy.

Quietly Grandma said, *"I hope someone's keeping track of what's in the bag for when I write the thank-you note."*

That's Grandma. She hasn't really been able to write for a while, but her first thought is still of others.

Somehow talk shifted to how nicely Grandma wakes up when someone awakens her. Grandpa reminded Mom of how unhappily she woke up as a teenager . . . perhaps because Grandma woke her up by blowing in her face.

"Grandma! You blew in her face?"

"Well, I didn't have halitosis."

"I don't blame you for being grumpy, Mom!"

"Or she would run her fingers lightly over my face."

"Grandma!!"

Grandma just chuckled at the memory.

Thursday, February 13

Conversations are getting harder. Grandma tires so easily. And while she is still very much in the moment it's a struggle to recall the preceding moments. Time overwhelms her more and more. If she's feeling well enough, she can still slip back into the past, but the effort of putting the words together is sometimes more than she can muster.

So I hold her hand and tell her how loved she is and how many people—some who haven't met her but feel like they know her—are praying for her. And I stroll through her memories alone while she dozes beside me.

We only had fresh beef once a year when the butchering was done. We never had veal. Dad thought it was wrong to pen calves up like that, so he wouldn't do it. But cows got butchered. Mom canned the beef. And the pork chops went in big crocks full of lard down in the basement. I loved when Mom would send me down to get the pork chops out. I loved the feeling of the lard running through my fingers.

Mom canned all kinds of things. We grew mostly grains on the farm: wheat, oats, rye, corn. But we had a garden, too. Mom canned the vegetables. Those stayed upstairs in the pantry, but the other things—meat, potatoes, apples— went down in the basement. It was just earthen with a little stream running through it, and it was cold.

We grew the best lettuce. It was to die for. And Mom would cut it up and sprinkle vinegar and sugar on it. I loved it.

And the sweet peas. They were my favorite.

There used to be a big tree out in one of the pastures. Probably an oak. You could see it out the kitchen window. I loved that tree. Once I came home for a weekend and the tree was gone. I was just sick. It broke my heart. I loved that tree. I guess it got diseased and they had to cut it down.

The schoolhouse was on the edge of our property. It was my job to tend the fire. But I didn't want the other children to know, so I went very early before school started. It was a real job, I got paid. I gave the money to Mom. I never thought about keeping it—what would I have done with money?

Sometimes the boys would play baseball. Once when I was maybe ten John came home from playing and left his things out. I asked him what was on top, and he told me it was a hat. So I put it on my head and wore it around. I thought I was so classy. It was a jock strap. I didn't know.

At recess we'd play pum-pum-pullaway in the schoolyard. But there was one boy—Monte Ferguson—who would never be It. I would tag him, and he'd say, "you didn't touch me. You touched my shirt."

And I'd say, "I did too touch you!"

He made me so mad!

Sometimes Floretta would invite me to spend the night at her house. And I always wanted to. But when it would be time to get ready for bed, I wouldn't want to stay. The house was so dusty. Mrs. McNitt was not a housekeeper like Mom. I'd see all that dust, and then I'd say I had to go home. I don't think I ever actually spent the night there.

On Sundays—if my brothers and sisters didn't come home for the weekend—John would run Mom and me into Conklin for church. He didn't stay. And Dad didn't go. He read the Bible to himself in the evenings.

Friday, February 14—Valentine's Day

As I hold my three-week old nephew I want him to know he is safe, he is loved, he is not alone, he is a gift. And as I hold my grandma's hand I want her to know she is safe, she is loved, she is not alone, she is a gift.

I am privileged to be present on the edges of their journeys—one beginning, one ending. And I find myself telling them the same things: I love you, I love you, I love you; my life is richer because you are in it.

I want to memorize each fraction of each second. The dance on the outskirts of life slips away before I'm ready. So I trace my finger along their delicate hands. I study the line of their cheekbones. I etch their profiles on the inner canvas of my mind. I celebrate each successful meal and try not to fret over the rate of ounces lost or gained. I smile and speak softly as they awaken and struggle to make sense of their surroundings. I breathe a sigh of relief when recognition flickers through their eyes or they relax at my touch.

And as each day draws to a close I am spent with gratitude. Another day. Another opportunity to love. Another chance to be present.

I was made for this.

Monday, February 17

Time slips and slides. Even with a clock on the wall listing the date and day of the week along with the time, it's too hard to track when the walls look the same and the patterns lose logic: naps between meals, visitors and nurses at random times. The lines between day and night and day again blur into continuous twilight.

Grandma tries, but it's elusive. *"Did you have a good weekend?"*

"It's Friday evening, so it's starting off well."

We repeat this conversation throughout my Friday visit.

"How's your week going?"

43

"I had a good week. And now I'm having a good weekend. Tonight Mom and Dad and I are going to dinner and an opera at Biola with Aunt Jill, Uncle Brian and Jessica."

"Oh, it's the weekend."

We cycled through that exchange every few minutes on Saturday.

Sometimes frustration flickers through Grandma's eyes in the moments she realizes we've been down this road. But often we just repeat as though it's the first time. And it's new all over again.

How do I help measure time when it's lost all meaning? I hear myself saying unhelpful things like "I'll be back soon—I'll see you tomorrow" in the same conversation with "They'll be here soon—just a week and a half until Lennie and Kathy arrive." Really, Kristen? "Soon" for one day and ten days? And while I know neither comment sticks I want to find a way to add meaning, not further diminish it.

But even as time blurs, Grandma rallies. Her weight is slipping—down to 91 pounds—but she was able to get out of her wheelchair and walk with minimal help to the bathroom twice in two hours today. A strength she didn't have even a few days ago. Not only did she walk, but she sat up and talked for hours without needing a nap.

She was nauseous when lunch arrived, so I thought we could focus on drinking her Ensure to try to get maximum calories as easily as possible. I didn't even mention the food, but after a few minutes she picked up her fork and ate three bites. It didn't taste good to her, but for the first time in five and a half weeks Grandma fed herself!

Wednesday, February 19

Yesterday was my one day of the week I didn't make it to see Grandma. Not getting to see her was eating at me, so as I left work and headed to my brother's house to spend a little time with my niece and nephew I called Mom. She was still with Grandma.

"Would you tell her I'm sorry I don't think I'll make it there today, but I will definitely be there tomorrow? And will you tell her I love her, I love her, I love her?"

"Or you could tell her."

Mom gave Grandma the phone.

"*Hi, Honey.*"

"Hi, Grandma. I'm not sure if I can make it by to see you before I go to Bible Study tonight."

"*Okay. I'm sure you'll do your best.*"

"But I'll definitely be there tomorrow!"

"*Oh, good.*"

"I miss you! And I love you, I love you, I love you."

"*I love you, I love you, I love you. Bye-bye.*"

"Bye."

Later Mom and I talked about her visit. She said they'd had a great time talking about their time in Georgia. Even though they didn't live there long, it held a lot of memories for each of them. When Mom mentioned that she'd love to go back some day, Grandma agreed that would be nice, but cautioned that when you go back, it's never the same . . . and sometimes it can be disappointing.

I know about that time in Mom and Grandma's life, but I don't really know about it. Georgia was a new beginning and an ending. And while Mom and Grandma have always been willing to talk about it, the conversations usually stay on the safer, happier memories.

"So when exactly did you move to Georgia?"

"The summer between kindergarten and first grade. Probably that August—"

That would have been 1958.

"—and we were there not quite a year and a half. Or maybe less. I went to all of first grade there. And I started second grade. We probably moved back around the end of October."

October 1959.

"Did you ever see your dad again after you got back to California?"

"Oh, yes! He'd pick me up and take me places. And they got back together for a while."

"They did?"

"Yes. When we moved back, my mom and I moved in with Aunt Grace and Uncle Rudy. I really don't know where my dad was living. He might have been in the apartment. I'm not sure. And then they decided to give it another shot. And we lived in an apartment. It didn't last very long. I really don't know how long. When they split for good—probably before the school year ended—my mom got an apartment so I could stay at the same school. I guess she figured three schools in second grade was hard enough."

"Three? One in Georgia, one while you were with Aunt Grace and Uncle Rudy and one when you moved back with your dad?"

"Yes. And I don't know if he stayed in that apartment then. I just don't remember. But he would pick me up and, well, he'd take me to bars. And then tell me not to tell Grandma."

"Seriously? Did you tell her?"

"I don't remember. It wasn't like—'Don't you tell your mother!' It wasn't like that. We probably went to a movie or something, and then he'd want a drink, so we'd stop at a bar. It was always in the afternoon. And he'd sit me on the bar and get me a Shirley Temple."

"Wow. Was he working then?"

"I don't think so."

"But he'd pay for everything."

A shrug.

"I don't remember all the details. But at some point Russ Smith had a friend, Joanie. I guess he knew her from college or something. And anyone the Smiths knew, we knew. We were always over there. And I don't know if she lived with us—we just had a one-bedroom apartment, maybe she did and slept on the couch—or what. She may have just been helping Grandma out. I really don't know. She took care of me after school, and maybe during the summer . . .

"My last memory of my father . . . oh, it was awful. He wanted to take me to the circus. And Grandma said okay, so he'd already bought the tickets. But I didn't want to go."

"Because you didn't want to go with him or because you didn't want to go to the circus?"

"Probably both. Things were just different then. Now someone would say, 'Oh, she doesn't want to go, don't make her go with him.' But Grandma said he'd already paid for it. I had to go. And I said I'd feel better if Joanie could go. So I don't know if Grandma called him or what, but he wasn't happy about it. And he said she couldn't sit with us—he already bought our tickets and they were assigned seats—and I said that was okay. So I guess he bought her a ticket. It must have been the summer between second and third grade because it was during the day, and I wouldn't have missed school for the circus . . . That's my last memory."

The summer of 1960. The summer Mom turned eight. The last time she saw her biological father.

It would be a little over three years later after Grandma remarried—but a few years before Mom was adopted by her stepdad—a knock on the door would deliver the news that on November 22, 1963, Joseph Gutweiler died on skid row at the age of 54. Cirrhosis of the liver. The day of one of the most famous deaths in American history another man died in obscurity on the streets of Los Angeles.

Thursday, February 20

Grandma was cold and Mom was wrapping more blankets around her when I walked in on Thursday. I was burning up, so she wrapped her icy hands around my forearms and slowly moved them up and down my arms marveling at how I could be so warm. I thanked her for cooling me off, and she laughed about what a pair we were. And soon she was laughing at what a klutz I was as I whacked my own elbow on the back of my own chair.

"There is someone out there who wants a partner like you," Grandma laughed.

That's an uncharacteristic comment. I don't think Grandma has ever once commented on or questioned me about my singleness . . . or really any major facet of my life. Not that she doesn't care, just that it never mattered. She never defined me that way. She's always loved me just as I am and never thought I've needed to be or do anything different. She's always made me feel complete. She's always believed in me. She's always been proud of me. Working, unemployed, single, with a plan, without a plan—it's never mattered. She loves me for who I am, not what I'm doing.

Well, almost, she has been mentioning how it's not too late for me to become a nurse. But I don't think that really counts.

After Mom left, Grandma and I kept talking. Out of the blue she brought up Leonard. He'd been on my mind, too. I'd been running through her siblings and trying to remember stories about each of them, and I realized Leonard's name didn't come up very often.

"I don't really know much about Uncle Leonard. What was he like?"

"Leonard was a great guy. But he had a temper. Mom used to warn him about his temper. She'd say, 'That temper. If you aren't careful, it's going to be trouble for you.'

"He got in a brawl with another boy once. I don't know if they both wanted to take the same girl to a dance or what. But they went at it. And then they just stopped and shook hands and that was that.

"One time when I was about ten we were at the Grange for a dance. They wouldn't leave me at home by myself. Leonard didn't really like ballroom dancing. He preferred . . . what do you call it . . . Polish? I don't know. Leonard had a date, but he came over and got me and danced me all over that hall. I thought I had the world in my grasp."

The memories got a little harder to follow for a while. Generations blurred and the timeline lost its scale.

"Did all of your siblings always stay close when you all grew up?"

"No. Not always. I think Bill was the black sheep. He was kind of shut out by the others, but he came back later in life. I think they were all close then."

She was getting tired, and it was getting harder for her to sit up in the wheelchair.

"Grandma, would you like to get back in bed?"

"Well, what would you do?"

"I'd sit right next to you and we'd keep talking."

"You won't leave?"

"No, I won't leave. I'll stay right here."

"Well, that might be nice."

After the nurse helped her into the bathroom she hesitated on getting back in bed. I assured her I wouldn't leave if she lay down, I'd be right next to her. Even the nurse was trying to set her mind at ease that I would stay whether she was sitting up or in bed.

Lupe got her settled in bed, and I stayed and held her hand until Grandpa arrived to help her with dinner.

"I'm going to go now, but I'll be back tomorrow, okay?"

"I just lit up when I saw you coming in . . . yesterday was kind of a low day."

"Yesterday was a low day?"

"Yes."

"You got to play Euchre with Mom and Uncle Brian and Grandpa yesterday. You and Mom even won."

"Oh."

"I'm sorry it was a low day. Is today a better day?"

"I think so."

"I'm glad. Hopefully tomorrow will be another better day. I'm going to try to get into work early tomorrow so I can get here sooner, okay? I'll get here as soon as I can."

"Okay. I love you, Sweetheart."

"I love you, too!"

Friday, February 21

Grandma had that faraway look today. Grandpa and the hospice nurses think she's depressed. And I don't doubt it, but she's the most gracious depressed person. It almost makes it harder, she's still trying to take care of us and make it easier on us, when all we want is to make it better for her.

Mom and I did most of the talking. Grandma corrected when we got the details out of order, but she had less to say than most days.

"It'd be good to run those roads again," she sighed.

And then she was gone, lost in the waves of time. She spoke of her mom as though she were still alive, and she talked about what her mom thought of her grandson Jack's troubled marriages—except of course Grandma Borgman didn't live to know Jack's wives.

"She would just bite her lip and not interfere in her children's lives."

A pained look crossed Mom's eyes. It's hard to help Grandma navigate these murky waters.

After Mom left and the nurse got Grandma comfortably back in bed, I leaned over to fix Grandma's oxygen. It wasn't actually in her nose any more.

"Let me get that for you . . . it was funny."

"I must have a funny nose."

"Your nose is just perfect."

"You'd cover every which way for me."

"I would."

She smiled at me. She's right, there's nothing I wouldn't do for her. And truly she can do no wrong in my eyes.

"You can close your eyes, Grandma."

"But what will you do?"

"I'll be right here."

"For like fifteen minutes?"

"As long as you want."

"Okay, see you in a few minutes."

It is stunning how quickly she can go to sleep. In less than a minute she was breathing heavily. She never heard Mrs. Wong greet me as she wheeled into the room or the alarm sounding in the hallway or the clatter when something fell from Mrs. Wong's tray.

I watched her sleep, and then pulled out a book, *Berlin Diary* by William Shirer. When Grandma's eyes flickered open she was surprised to see me.

"Hi, Honey—you look so beautiful sitting there. And here I'm sleeping."

She clearly didn't remember I was still here. No memory of our time before she fell asleep. She thinks I just got here while she was sleeping.

"I told you I'd be here when you woke up. You just had a little nap, and I'm still right here."

"How long did I sleep?"

"About a half an hour."

"Oh, I feel like I've been asleep for ages. I think if I put my eyes to half mast I'd be asleep in half a second."

"Then why don't you do that? I need to get home for dinner, and Grandpa will be here in about fifteen minutes, and then dinner will be here. You could sleep until then . . . And I'll be back tomorrow—I'm not sure just when, but I promise I'll be here tomorrow."

"That's a promise I like."

"I love you, I love you, I love you."

"I love you, I love you, I love you."

Sunday, February 23

The tears start leaking out. I roll onto my back. They run down the side of my face and off my right earlobe into the hair and pillow. On the left side they miss the earlobe and begin to pool in my ear canal. I don't care. At least something is full. I fell like I've been gutted. Hollowed. My arms are wrapped around me clutching fistfuls of my pajamas. It's as though I'll break apart—come unhinged at the joints—if I dare let go.

An hour later my left nostril is whistling and the pain in my right sinus is snaking around my eye. I don't cry well.

My fingertips ache from pressing into my palms through the fabric. My nails feel as though they're pushing back into their beds, but I can't let go.

I don't even know why I'm crying.

Is it because Grandma fell yesterday? She was trying to get to the dresser where the pictures of her family are. Was she trying to get to us?

Is it because she was alone slumped over asleep in her wheelchair in an empty room when I got there today? And then as we were talking she nodded toward the wall and said, *"I must look at that picture of your folks twenty times a day. Ed looks like Ed, but I can't figure out who you look like?"*

Does she think I'm my mom? Did I shift from Kristen to Joanne in a sentence? It doesn't matter, but I want to respond correctly. I hate it when she realizes she's slipped. I will be whomever I need to be or repeat a conversation however many times she wants, but it kills me when she realizes she's mixed something up or re-traveled the same conversational ground.

But I don't know if that's why I'm crying now. I'm not even sure if there is a reason or if my soul hit an arbitrary capacity. There was no provocation. One minute waiting for sleep to come. The next tears. I tried to pray them away, but I don't even know how to do that any more. What do I pray? How do I pray? Beyond begging for her to be safe and feel loved each moment until she reaches the ultimate safety and love of heaven, what is the right prayer? Do I pray for her to get off hospice? Do I pray for her appetite to come back and her to want to eat? Do I pray for her to remember her visitors and where she is? Do I pray for energy and strength? Or do I pray for her to sleep more of the day away? Do I pray for us to be able to keep her longer or for her to be freed from her tiring body? I don't know. And when all I can do is pray, it feels like a copout to rely on the Spirit to fill in the places my words are lacking. I'm muted when all I had left was words.

So my pillow becomes soggy, and necessity forces my hands to unclench to use my pajama sleeves to wipe my nose. And I don't care. I don't care that I'm using hair and pillows and pajamas for Kleenex because all I really want to do is hold my grandma in my arms and tell her I love her so much it hurts.

I should get up and blow my nose, change my shirt, get a new pillow . . . but I'd rather curl up into a ball and figure out how many hours I have to make it until I can see her again, how soon I can hear her voice, hold her hand. It's her presence I desperately want—that's the cure for the tears. And not knowing how many more opportunities I have to be present with her starts the tears all over again.

And so I sing. In my head I loop through a broken medley. My musical amnesia keeps me from remembering all the words or tunes—I just string them together however I can . . .

. . . When peace like a river attendeth my soul / when sorrows like sea billows roll / whatever my lot / Thou hast taught me to say, 'It is well, it is well with my soul'

. . . This is the day that the Lord has made / I will rejoice and be glad in it

. . . Great is Thy faithfulness / morning by morning new mercies I see / all I have needed Thy hand hath provided / Great is Thy faithfulness Lord unto me

. . . O Lord my God, when I in awesome wonder / consider all the worlds Thy hands have made/ I see the stars, I hear the rolling thunder / Thy power throughout the universe displayed / Then sings my soul, My Savior God, to Thee / How great Thou art / How great Thou art

. . . The sun comes up, it's a new day dawning / It's time to sing Your song again / Whatever may pass and whatever lies before me / Let me be singing when the evening comes / Bless the Lord, O my soul / O my soul / Worship His holy name / Sing like never before

. . .'Tis so sweet to trust in Jesus / just to take Him at His word / just to rest upon His promise / just to know 'thus says the Lord' / Jesus, Jesus, how I trust Him / How I've proved Him o'er and o'er / Jesus, Jesus, precious Jesus / O for grace to trust Him more

Monday, March 3

Lennie and Kathy arrived last Wednesday for five days. Even though we know the Michigan stories, it's different having Michiganders here. They spent hours each day sitting with her and talking. Lennie reminisced about his own childhood memories of Grandma—his Aunt Max—visiting and his trips to Conklin to visit his grandparents.

"Aunt Max, did Aunt Sally play the guitar?"

"No. But she had one."

"But she didn't play?"

"I don't think so. I think she just had it to, you know, set her apart. To make her different."

I thought of how Grandma has described her sister, Sally, as being a bit plain with weak eyes. She didn't stand out in a crowd—or a large family.

Lennie continued, "One time when I was little my dad took Ruth and me out to Grandpa and Grandma's, and he and Uncle Byron and I were out in the barn poking around. And I remember there was this great big safe on wheels and this guitar they said was Aunt Sally's."

"Probably."

When Grandma was telling a story about Lennie's dad Leonard at the dances, I asked him if that sounded like his dad.

"I never saw him dance."

"Well he wasn't much of a dancer. He didn't care for it, but he did like square dancing. Not ballroom or anything. But he would ask me to dance, and

I was just on cloud nine."

Lennie just smiled and shook his head. A version of his dad he'd never really known.

Leonard died in 1984 at the age of seventy-four. He had a massive heart attack one day most likely from the stress of caring for his wife who had early onset Alzheimer's and his mother-in-law who had dementia. Kathy said he'd been covering for Ruby's slips for years. Aunt Jane—Uncle John's wife—delivered the news unceremoniously to Lennie over the phone, "Lennie, your dad's dead."

Lennie and Kathy took in his mom. But after a month of caring for their own young sons, his mother with Alzheimer's and Kathy's grandma with dementia, it was too much. They moved his mother, Ruby, into a skilled nursing facility to be cared for the last nine years of her life.

Though Grandma moved to California when she was twenty-two—and really only lived near two nieces and one nephew when they were very young—she was always a presence in their lives, even from a distance.

One of Lennie's fondest childhood memories was getting to ride from Muskegon to Chicago with Aunt Sally to take Aunt Max back to the airport. And they got him ice cream.

Even when she and I visited in 1998, her nieces and nephews—and great-nieces and great-nephews—couldn't wait to see her. They were happy to meet me, but it was Aunt Max they all wanted to be with. It felt like being with a celebrity.

It's the presence phenomenon. Grandma has a way of being fully present. She is fully in the moment, in the conversation, in the room—whoever is with her feels he or she is the only person in the world. Grandma was an active listener before people paid good money to learn how to listen and ask clarifying questions to check for understanding. She is a good conversationalist, but she is a great listener. I don't think Grandma has ever been so eager to make her next comment she's stopped listening to the person talking to her. She doesn't monopolize conversations or play conversational one-upmanship. She listens with empathy and celebrates or mourns as appropriate.

As I go each day to see Grandma, it's my privilege to be present.

I ask questions, and I listen. I ride wherever she wants to steer the conversation. I hold her hand and hold her gaze. I don't worry about what's already happened in the day or week, and I don't think about what I have left to do later. This is the moment I have to be present, and the next one will take care of itself in its time.

I can't worry about the hours I'm not with Grandma, but I can focus on loving her fully while I am with her. Love is like presence. I can't love in the past—that opportunity is gone. And I can't plan on loving in the future—that opportunity hasn't come. But I can love right now.

Sunday, March 9

I brought a guest book with me today. Grandma is the most loved person I know, but time is deceiving her and she can't remember who has been visiting with her or when they came.

Earlier this week she told Marge and Carol that Mom only visits about once a week, though she's there six or seven days a week—every week.

So I date the first line of the book and write my name. Mom and Dad add theirs. Before I leave the Barberos are there. Soon Grandpa will be down, and later Jon and Angela and Norah will visit. I don't know if it will work, but maybe seeing the names will help jog her memory of her many, many visitors each day and remind her in the rare solitary moments that tend to chase the memories of companionship away that she is neither forgotten nor abandoned.

She's getting stronger. After dipping to 91 pounds, she's rallied to almost 100 just two weeks later. She feeds herself now and eats not only her meals but also all the treats we smuggle in to her.

Yet with strength and energy comes restlessness and frustration. Three days ago they added an alarmed seatbelt to her wheelchair. Ever the hostess, she kept trying to get up to welcome people and see them out. But her legs have joined forces with her mind and betray her intentions. The staff is concerned she'll fall.

She hates the belt. When I arrived yesterday, poor Yodet was standing next to her in a state of bewilderment. Somehow Grandma had not only unbelted herself, but re-belted it behind her to silence the alarm. She was getting agitated as Yodet tried to determine how she freed herself.

"Grandma, you're quite the Houdini, aren't you?" I asked with a smile as I knelt in front of her.

I reached around her and grabbed the belt, which Yodet snapped into place. I asked, "Can you show me how you undo this?"

She reached down and grasped each side. With unexpected strength she depressed the button and took it off. The alarm began sounding.

"Then what do you do?" Yodet asked.

With quiet defiance, Grandma said, *"I don't know. I didn't do anything."*

"I know you don't like the belt—"

"I hate it."

"—okay, you hate the belt, but we want you to be safe. No one wants you to fall, so we want to make sure there's always someone with you when you get up. That's why it's important to always call someone to help you when you want to go to the bathroom." Even as I tried to make the words sound casual I cringed at how her dignity and independence was being stripped away moment by moment.

"I can get there by myself. I can't spend the rest of my life like this."

I swallowed hard. "And no one wants you to. You're getting so much stronger, but your legs are still a little weak. If you keep eating well, hopefully you can start therapy soon and practice walking. And then you won't have to have the belt any more, and you can move around however you want."

She nodded.

I held her hand to keep her fingers from fidgeting with the belt, but I can't blame her for despising its presence.

When I arrived today Dad showed me a note Grandpa left us. It said we were allowed to un-belt Grandma while we there as long as we put it back on her when we left.

As I prepared to leave her with the Barberos today, I leaned in to kiss her.

"I'll see you tomorrow, okay?"

"Okay."

"I know you don't like it, but I have to put your belt back on before I go," I said as I unfastened it from behind her back, pulled it in front of her and clicked it in place.

"I hate that thing."

"I know. I'm very sorry, but it's to keep you safe. As soon as we can we'll take it off for good . . . I'll see you tomorrow. I love you!"

"I love you, Honey."

Sunday, March 16

On Monday the hospice nurse, Irene, confirmed Grandma didn't qualify for hospice. She was too healthy and death wasn't clinically imminent. But the insurance . . . she had to stay on hospice to stay in skilled nursing.

By Wednesday Grandpa was calling Mom at work to tell her hospice care was ending on Friday, March 14. The new insurance that would allow her to stay in skilled nursing and even receive therapy wouldn't start until April 1. That left seventeen days of limbo. And so she had to move.

Both Wednesday and Thursday she was fretful when I arrived. While the dementia makes remembering recent details difficult, it has not robbed her of her ability to read and recall emotion. She knew Grandpa was agitated. She knew people were worried and worked up about something, and she was pretty sure it was her. She boiled it down to "they" were unhappy with her.

"Who, Grandma?"

"They are. There's five of them."

"No one is upset with you."

"Yes they are," she said with rare tone.

"There's a lot going on right now, but you haven't done anything, and no one is upset with you. These are good changes. You're going to be able to start practicing walking more. You're getting stronger and stronger. Pretty soon you'll be able to do more yourself. I know you don't like having people have to help you."

"I don't."

Grandma hasn't understood she hasn't been home this whole

time. I didn't know how to tell her she's moving home when she thought she was home. For weeks she's been vaguely perturbed as to where Grandpa disappears to when he leaves her. What she perceives as him leaving home is in fact him going home. Confusion passes through her expression when he goes to eat in the dining hall and her meals are delivered to her. And she finally admitted this week she doesn't know where he's sleeping these days. When she worries I won't be able to find her, it must be because she can't find herself. She has no idea where she is, so how could I?

Mom and I took a walk Thursday evening. As we watched the sky put on a show in muted and then vivid pinks, we talked about Grandma and Grandpa. It's been an eye-opening few months. After watching Grandpa seem to grow in patience and compassion these past few years while Grandma has struggled a bit with her memory, he's seemed more . . . selfish since Grandma got sick.

He doesn't engage with her. He says insensitive things. He talks down to her or about her in her presence. There is not a thing wrong with her hearing.

When Grandma was in the hospital and it looked like maybe she was healthy enough to go to rehab, Grandpa said she would never live in his apartment again. He wanted her on hospice. From moment one he wanted to make sure she had a DNR and it was very, very clear no heroic measures would be taken. He told everyone who would listen she wanted to be allowed to die.

But she didn't die. And she's blown everyone's expectations out of the water. Two and a half months shy of her ninetieth birthday she is eating better than she's eaten in years. She gets stronger by the day. And while the dementia takes much from her, it has revealed the depth of her character: her graciousness, her humility, her selflessness, her ability to see and believe good in everyone.

Friday arrived.

Grandma graduated from hospice, and because of the insurance conundrum, she moved home to their apartment with 24-hour caregivers.

I arrived shortly after she did—and after Mom went home, Grandpa went to dinner and Uncle Brian went home—it was just Grandma, her caregiver Jessica and me.

Grandma was sitting with her feet up in her La-Z-Boy covered in an unzipped sleeping bag to keep her warm. Grandpa was picking up a walker after he ate dinner, so when Grandma's dinner arrived, I thought we only had to get her a few feet from the chair to the table.

As I arranged her dinner and started her coffee, Jessica began to get her up. And Grandma said, *"Well, I just need to make a pit stop first."*

My eyes met Jessica's. The bathroom was at least twenty feet away . . . each way. We had no wheelchair and no walker. Jessica nodded. She and I each took a side and began walking with Grandma to the bathroom.

For someone who hasn't walked in more than six weeks, she did well and was completely unfazed at her accomplishment. By the time she made it to the dinner table, she was a little tired but dug right into her food as though nothing extraordinary had taken place.

By yesterday she was using her walker like a pro—letting go and reaching for tables or chairs a little before I was comfortable, but thankfully her caregivers were always right on top of it.

Today I got there after church. Grandpa let me in and introduced me to April Romo who will be the primary daytime caregiver. Grandma slept peacefully in her chair through Grandpa's booming voice and April's quiet hello. But as soon as I said hi, her head shot up, her eyes opened and she said, *"I heard a voice."*

"Hi, Grandma."

"Oh, hi, Honey."

A football movie was playing on the TV, and as I sat by Grandma I could see her struggling to care—she's an avid baseball fan, but other sports don't really interest her and movie plotlines are hard for her to follow.

"Grandma? I was wondering if you might want to play a game."

"Oh?"

"I was thinking maybe we could play Farkle."

"Oh, we could."

"Grandpa, where are the Farkle dice and some paper?"

"Right in there," he pointed toward the bedroom, "in the top drawer of her nightstand."

Of course, where else would games be? Grandma's entire drawer was full of dice, decks of cards, Cribbage boards, pads of paper with various games in mid-score on them. And Kleenex. Games and Kleenex. Perfect.

For the next two hours Grandma, April and I played Farkle. We stopped for Grandma and April to eat their lunches when they arrived, but then we got right back to it. I won two games, and Grandma won one. Beginner's luck failed April, but she'll get a lot more practice in the days to come.

Sometimes the rules of the game or the strategy seemed to fade away for Grandma, but other times she was doing mental math faster than April or I and taking calculated risks that paid dividends.

She was pretty tired by the end of the third game, so she was heading to the bathroom and then to her recliner for a nap when I left for the day.

Seventeen days are down to fifteen. It's unclear if there's any chance she'll be able to stay in the apartment come April 1, but I will enjoy every moment of her being home. She's beaten the odds so far, and though these next odds seem a bit more contingent on Grandpa's willingness than Grandma's, I'm not sure anything can surprise me at this point. And come what come may, I will be as present as possible wherever Grandma is.

Monday, March 17—St. Patrick's Day

When Mom and I arrived after work today, Grandma was under her sleeping bag in the chair, but she was wearing pajamas.

After two long walks with her caregiver, including one outside, Grandma had showered and asked to get ready for bed. So she, Grandpa, Uncle Brian, Mom and I sat in the afternoon sunlight and talked about Conklin's record short St. Patrick's Day parade—less than a football field long—down Conklin's main drag ending in Fenian's Irish Pub.

The parade only started in 1987, so it didn't tie into Grandma's memories of Conklin, but given her father's occasional outings to the tavern back in her childhood, it seemed not at all surprising to her that the tiny town of Conklin would host St. Patrick's Day festivities that more than doubled the population with revelers.

Grandma's dad didn't drink often, but at least once when he didn't make it home from the tavern in time for supper, her mother locked him out. And somehow in the telling of the story it was always more about her mother's good sense of humor and ability to pull one over on her husband than the drinking.

As we chatted, Grandpa brought up how he talked to Lori—the head of skilled nursing—today and she promised there would be a bed for Grandma in skilled nursing on April 1.

Mom mentioned how well Grandma seemed to be doing since getting home and that hopefully she wouldn't need skilled nursing.

Grandpa moved beyond it, saying Lori would make sure she did a full evaluation on Grandma when she got back to skilled nursing . . . not much progress yet on Grandpa wanting Grandma to stay in the apartment. As we walked to our cars Uncle Brian said he would talk with Lori this week to find out the insurance and care details.

Could caregiving continue in their apartment if he would pay for it? What about both of them moving to assisted living?

Those are the questions I want answered. Those are the questions not only of logistics but of heart. Whose needs and desires are driving these decisions?

And who am I to question Grandpa's motivations and decisions? I've been so focused on what I want for Grandma and how I can love her . . . have I put myself in his shoes? Have I even tried to love him the way I'm loving her right now? She's easy to love. He's not so much. But didn't Jesus talk about that? What credit is it to love the lovable? Anyone can do that. Am I loving the less lovable, too?

Friday, March 21

Wednesday was the day. I woke up praying for Grandpa and Uncle Brian's dinner conversation—a conversation Grandpa didn't know was coming, but one that would be on my mind and heart all day. I fasted and prayed throughout the day. At lunch I spent my thirty minutes walking and praying, asking God to give wisdom and love-saturated words of truth to Uncle Brian and a soft heart and open ears to Grandpa.

Later that evening Uncle Brian came over to talk to Mom and me while Dad was at choir practice. His take on their conversation was that Grandpa isn't processing with much depth. As long as things seem smooth to him, then he's fine. He couldn't really answer what he's learning or how God might be asking him to love sacrificially through this, though maybe the seed has been planted. But most promising, he seemed open to the idea of he and Grandma staying together come April 1 and maybe even open to the possibility of them moving to assisted living.

After we talked and Uncle Brian and Mom decided they needed to go and talk directly to the staff themselves without Grandpa, we sat together and prayed. We prayed for Grandma. We prayed for Grandpa. We prayed for ourselves. We sought God's creativity in caring for Grandma. Nothing in the last two and a half months has gone as any of us would have anticipated or planned, I can't imagine we'll accurately predict how the next weeks and months will unfold.

Yesterday—Thursday—I walked in the door and was greeted by Aunt Jill in the kitchenette getting water for herself and Grandma. I grabbed a chair from the table and slid between Grandma's recliner and April's chair to fit into the circle between April and Uncle Brian. As I greeted everyone Grandma started trying to get up. She tries to climb out over the raised footrest of her La-Z-Boy, but once reminded she waits patiently for it to be put down. After her footrest had been lowered and her walker placed in front of her chair, she got up and headed for the door. She and April were off. I'm not sure she registered me as present before she was out and walking.

Even when they got back from a short walk in the hall, she seemed to struggle a bit to place me—until we were discussing favorite restaurants and Grandpa and I started talking about how she ate us both under the table at Hash House A Go Go when they visited me in Vegas five years ago. She grinned and laughed.

"I don't know what you are," Uncle Brian said to me.

"Oh, I think we do," Grandma replied.

"Oh? I might need a little help," Brian said.

"She's sharp. She's smart. I don't hold a . . ."

"Candle?" Grandpa offered.

"I don't hold a candle to what she can do."

"I don't know about that, Grandma . . . I bet you can still type faster than me!"

"Not. Any. More."

"You can do shorthand," Grandpa added.

"Oh, that's true—I could never do shorthand."

"You just never learned. I'm sure you could have."

"Her first job after she finished business college was at Continental Aviation as a secretary," Grandpa told April.

"It was a big plant."

"And this guy walked up and plopped himself right down on her desk. He asked her if she took shorthand, and she said yes. So he started going a mile a minute with all kinds of airplane parts and jargon, and then he stopped and told her to read it back to him.

"And she had to tell him she didn't get any of it. She didn't know any of those terms.

"So he went into her boss' office and started telling him. And that was a bad move. He got fired!" Grandpa said.

"I felt bad for him."

"It wasn't the first time he tried to make a fool of a new secretary. He thought mighty highly of himself," Grandpa added.

"He did think highly of himself."

After Uncle Brian and Aunt Jill left, Grandpa headed to dinner, and then Grandma and April and I chatted. Grandma's gaze kept drifting out the sliding door, but I couldn't see what she was seeing.

"Grandma, your amaryllis is doing so well—look how much more it's opened."

"Yes."

"How long do those flowers last?" April asked.

"I have no idea . . . I think a long time . . ." I glanced at Grandma, but she didn't seem to be paying attention to us.

"Grandma, did you have amaryllis at your house on Birchleaf?"

Blank look.

"In the planter as you walked up along the side of the garage?"

"You know, I don't remember."

"Did you have flowers on the farm?"

Huge smile. *"Oh, yes, Mother loved flowers! I don't think Dad really cared for them, but he'd dig the holes for them."*

"Were they by the house?"

"They were about half way between the house and the . . . what did we call that building? It was kind of like a shed . . . there was the house and then . . ." she motioned with her hands.

"There were the two barns."

"Yes."

"And the chicken coop."

"The chicken coop."

"There was something else besides the outhouse?"

"Oh, not the outhouse!"

Her hands settled in her lap.

"Sometimes my little cousin would come out to the farm. She was maybe ten or eleven, and she lived in the city. She would want to play with me, and I would play for a little while, but I had chores to do. So I'd tell her, 'Now we can play again later but I need to help Auntie Emma.' And then she would ask if she could help too, and I'd try to think of little projects for her. But she wasn't much help. She didn't like to get her hands dirty."

"Sounds like your sister Dollie—I mean—Verlyn. Wasn't she the one who didn't like to get her hands dirty?"

"Oh, Verlyn! Yes. She and her boyfriend would come on Thursday afternoons. That was her time off, and his too. And she would be all dressed and wearing heels. She'd get out of the car and pick her way across the grass in her heels trying not to step in the . . . bird . . . stuff. And Dollie and I thought it was just so funny. We could hardly keep from laughing. You know, Dollie and I never tried to not step in the bird stuff, and we never stepped in it. But Verlyn tried so hard in her heels, and she stepped in it every time."

"Grandma, was Verlyn's first job for the Wyants?"

Turning to April, *"Verlyn—the oldest girl in the family—went to work for the Wyants. They were so good to her. Mr. Wyant was a businessman. He owned just about all of Muskegon."*

"How old do you think Verlyn was when she started working for them?" I asked.

"Let me see . . . seventeen."

"Verlyn didn't finish high school, did she?"

"Oh no, I'm the only one who did."

"The only girl."

"Yes, the only girl. Dollie didn't even want to go!"

If Verlyn started working in town at seventeen, that would have been when Grandma was just a baby. She was off the farm before Grandma even remembers the farm. Verlyn probably did move to town as a teenager to work, though if it was for the Wyants at that time is less clear.

Numbers and time have become more and more illusive. A few weeks ago Grandma said, *"When I was talking to Dollie last week—well, not last week . . . you know, when she was alive."* And she went on to tell a story about her mother. But Dollie died almost fifteen years ago. Or when I asked Grandma how long she worked at Birds Eye and she matter-of-factly said, *"Eight years."* Yet in the same conversation she said she married Joe, Mom's dad, when she was twenty-three and he made her quit her job when they got married. And the truth is probably somewhere in the middle. She may have started at Birds Eye around twenty-one. But she didn't marry Joe until she was twenty-seven. She may have worked at Birds Eye for five years.

We roll with it and reshuffle the stories and people into their correct places as we gather bits and pieces. The names and details shift, but the picture slowly comes into focus in the retellings.

April helped Grandma to the bathroom, and then their dinners arrived. We got Grandma settled, lifted the lid and saw a plateful of whole Brussels sprouts and a chicken breast—not pureed. April grabbed the lid off her plate thinking she or the waiter accidentally swapped the plates, but no, there was another plate of un-pureed food.

I took off to the dining hall to find out what we needed to do. After Daisy—in shock and fury—disappeared into the kitchen, I waited until the sweet, young waiter reappeared with a new tray. He apologized as we walked out of the dining hall.

"I'm sorry. I'm still kind of a novice at reading those papers. It's my fault."

"It's okay, we were just surprised."

"How's she doing?"

"She's doing really well. She's getting a lot stronger every day."

"We miss her so much!" he blurted out. "We just miss her so much."

"She's pretty special."

"She is! Are you her granddaughter?"

"I am. I'm one of the lucky ones. And I live close enough to get to see her a lot!"

As we walked into the room he handed me the new plate for Grandma and quietly picked up the old one. He never took his eyes off Grandma the whole time. And when she caught his eye and thanked him, the biggest smile I've ever seen broke across his face.

April brought Grandma her coffee and then sat down next to her.

"Grandma, I'm going to go now, okay? You and April enjoy your dinners . . . do you want me to pray for dinner before I go?"

"Yes, please."

I crouched next to Grandma's chair and held her hand.

"Dear God, thank you so much for Grandma and how much stronger she's getting. Thank you that she's able to get up and out and walk. We ask that you continue to strengthen her and that you bless this food to Grandma and April's bodies. Please give Grandma a good night's sleep. Thank you for loving us so much. In your name, amen."

I felt April start to stir and opened my eyes, but then Grandma started to pray.

"And I want to thank you so much for these girls who take such good care of me. I know they're going overtime, and I appreciate it so much. They're so good to me. And I don't know what I'd do without them. Thank you for their care. We love you. In your precious name, amen."

"Amen." I squeezed her hand.

"Amen," April murmured.

"Okay, I'll see you tomorrow," I said as I leaned in for a kiss. "I love you."

"I love you, Honey."

"Bye, April, see you tomorrow."

"Bye."

Sunday, March 23

While Mom and I were there yesterday Grandpa's cell phone rang. He was at lunch, but I recognized the number, so I answered it. Steve and Julie wanted to know if Grandma would be up for a visit later in the afternoon.

When I told Grandma the Spykermans would be coming, she started to fret that she wasn't ready. We assured her she looked beautiful. She had on the light blue blouse and black slacks she'd picked out in the morning. She still had some lipstick on and her hair was nicely combed. She didn't believe us. April brought her a mirror and her lipstick. She took one look and sighed. The three of us protested she looked beautiful, but she reapplied her lipstick and dropped the subject.

I arrived after church today to find Grandma, Mom, Dad and April watching the movie *Hook* on TV. Grandpa returned from church, and he asked Mom if they could talk. They had a long talk in the bedroom.

Grandpa and Mom discussed what might happen on April 1. According to Grandpa, Grandma has to go to skilled nursing. She will again be restrained in a wheelchair since they're worried about her trying to get up on her own. But she will get physical therapy to work on being able to get up from a chair or out of bed safely. And they'll evaluate her eating and try to reintroduce finely chopped food and eventually solid foods.

It seems Grandpa does want Grandma in the apartment, but at this point she doesn't meet the requirements. Even when she is more stable getting up and down and all around, and when she can handle a more textured diet, Grandpa might still need help; but we can't know that now.

I'm worried about moving her again. Every move has taken a toll on her spirit. But I understand the necessity. And Grandpa told Mom they've been discussing it and Grandma is aware of the move.

After their conversation, Dad and Mom headed out. Grandpa, Grandma, April and I finished the movie.

"Did you like that?" Grandpa asked Grandma.

"I couldn't hear a thing. I have no idea what was going on."

Grandma's hearing is fine, but the fast-moving, crowded scenes were far more than she could track.

Goonies was coming on next. "What's *Goonies*?" Grandpa asked.

"I don't know, I never saw it."

"You didn't see it?"

"No. I know Molly loved it when we were kids, but I never saw it."

"Did you watch much TV when you were growing up?" April asked.

"Not really. And definitely not a lot of movies—we didn't get a VCR until I was in eighth grade," I replied. "Grandpa and Grandma had a VCR way before we did. One of the many treats of going to their house: movies, soda, cookies, cake. At home, getting to stay up on Thursday nights and watch *The Cosby Show* was the big highlight of TV-viewing."

Grandpa switched on March Madness while we waited an hour for the Angels game to start. He left for lunch, and when Grandma and April's lunches arrived, we moved to the table.

Grandma was quiet as she ate before finally looking between the two of us, *"No one has anything to say?"*

"I guess we're duds," I replied.

"Well, I'm not touching that one."

"Do you have any stories for us? I bet you have one we don't know . . . but I don't know what to ask about to get the ones I don't know."

Grandma wandered through some memories of her siblings and how much she enjoyed growing up on a farm. She talked about how she had no regrets even though it was often a hard life and they didn't have much materially.

"I think everyone should get the chance to live like that for a portion of their lives."

It's an interesting thought. Not one of the eight surviving children in her family stayed on the farm. And of the five who had children, none had more than three children—no big families. Each of them raised their families in "the city."

When she paused and seemed lost in her thoughts, I asked, "Grandma? I've seen the pictures of your wedding to Grandpa. I can't remember the name of the church, but I remember the pictures. But where did you get married to Mom's dad? Was that in L.A.? Was it a church? The courthouse?"

She thought for a moment, *"The Grange Hall in Conklin."*

"You married Mom's dad in Conklin?"

"Yes."

"Was your family there?"

"Yes."

"Was his family there? Wasn't he from St. Louis?"

"What? The first one."

"There was someone before mom's dad, right?"

"Yes."

"And you married him in Conklin."

"Yes."

"What was his name? I know you've told me, but I can't remember."

"Oh, you're making my brain work so hard."

"Did you move out here to California with him?"

"No. It didn't work out."

Grandma has only mentioned her first marriage to me once before. It was around the time she and I went to Michigan in 1998 when I finished high school. I was trying to make a family tree to give myself some context for all the relatives I would meet, and when I asked about Grandma's first husband—meaning my mom's dad— she said a name I'd never heard. In my confusion I asked who he was, and she laughed and asked how I thought she got to California. Since then I always assumed they moved here after their wedding and the marriage dissolved here. Then she stayed and met Mom's dad while working at Birds Eye. But those years of her early twenties are a little murkier now.

"But you know, I wouldn't change it. Even the one that didn't work out. I wouldn't change a thing in my life."

Wednesday, March 26

Yesterday afternoon my cell phone rang at work. Mom and Uncle

Brian had been meeting with Lori Bond, the head of skilled nursing, to try to better understand the process and options come April 1. My heart leapt when I heard Mom's tone. And even while cautioning against excitement, Mom relayed Lori's opinion that Grandma seems like she may be too healthy for skilled nursing. She wants to do an evaluation before moving her to see if skilled nursing is the right fit or if perhaps it would make more sense for both Grandpa and Grandma to move to assisted living. Grandma would probably still need some additional caregiving, but she should qualify for in-home physical therapy, if she can go to assisted living.

Pure joy.

Even as I tried to rein it in, the possibility of limiting the number of times Grandma has to be moved—and the possibility of avoiding skilled nursing—was more than I had dared to hope.

It's far from a done deal, but Lori happened to see Grandma walking in the hall the other day and was so surprised by how well she was doing and how far she was able to walk, though she is still concerned about Grandma attempting to get out of bed unassisted.

The dementia has progressed over the past few months, and Grandma needs almost constant cuing. She tries to climb over the raised footrest of her La-Z-Boy before it's lowered. Whatever time she awakens she tries to get up and get ready for the day whether it's 10:30 p.m., 3:00 a.m. or 7:00 a.m. Her body is strengthening and remembering its routines, but her mind is not always able to keep pace.

With surging spirits I headed over for my daily visit.

When Grandma sat down at the table for dinner she tried to drink her fruit. "Do you want a spoon for that?" I asked.

"I thought I could drink it."

"Or you could drink it," I conceded.

But it was a bit thick, and drinking out of the scalloped dish didn't work. Undeterred she picked up a spoon and ate it all. She then set it back on her tray, bowed her head and began to pray aloud. April froze behind me, and I bowed my head.

"Precious Heavenly Father, thank you for today. Thank you so much for these girls who take care of me. As they head off in different directions, please bring them home safely. Thank you for taking such good care of us, and I just

appreciate what everyone in this building has done for me. As they go in different directions, please bring them home safely. And, Lord, I'm so thankful for these girls . . . and for Art. I'm appreciative of his care for me and his protection. Thank you for how these girls care for me. I love them so much. As they head off in different directions, please bring them home safely. Thank you for this food, and thank you for your love for us. In your precious name, amen."

April and I added our amens.

Later Tuesday night—still floating on the euphoria of Grandma's brighter prognosis—Mom greeted me with the news that Aunt Pat died.

I knew she'd gone on hospice and into a care facility recently, but when Aunt Jill and Uncle Brian saw her a few weeks ago they thought she looked and sounded good. I wasn't prepared for today.

The highs and the lows come so close together.

Mourning Aunt Pat is laced with relief she is freed from pain and present with Jesus, but it's a shock. As we advance and retreat and dance close to the finish line of Grandma's journey, I failed to grasp the more rapidly approaching lines of others.

Today, my joy over Grandma's news was dampened. Grandpa—who doesn't know about Mom and Uncle Brian's meeting with Lori—emailed the two of them to tell them that he's planning on moving out of their one-bedroom apartment and into a studio apartment to save money. He'll still hire extra caregivers for the night shift for Grandma in skilled nursing, but if she's able to leave skilled nursing, there won't be room for her in his apartment.

How do I begin to process news like that? What does it mean that he's choosing to move somewhere she can't be? Where is the fight for what's most compassionate and best for her? Is he even willing to entertain the idea of moving to assisted living together?

On an emotional scale of one to ten I hold pretty steady in the five to seven range . . . then the last two days I've rocketed and plummeted far out of my even-keeled norm. And yet, as I sputtered incoherent fragments of prayer, the quiet voice kept whispering, "Let go. My plans are better than yours. Have I not been faithful each step?"

And my soul settles.

He has been faithful. He has compassionately and creatively

provided beyond what I could imagine. And He will continue to . . . whether it fits with my hopes and expectations or not.

I held Grandma's hand as long as I could, and then later I held my two-month old nephew and listened to him wheeze—the circle pulled tighter. The delicate beginnings and endings. The desire to wrap my arms around those I love and whisper in their ears, "I love you, I love you, I love you. It's going to be okay."

Whatever okay is.

Thursday, March 27

Another day, another spin on the emotional rollercoaster.

All day at work I mulled my inability to wrap logic around a situation fluid with nuanced emotions, generational differences, familial intricacies and new medical ground for all of us.

I was antsy to get to Grandma's.

When I got there it was just Grandma and Cam—after eleven or so straight days, April had a day off today—watching the news. Grandma sketched the day and Cam colored in the details. Two big walks and a visit from Uncle Brian before he took Grandpa out for coffee.

And apparently two assessments. An LVN and a physical therapist watched Grandma get up and down and walk. They gave pointers for Grandma to practice, which Cam was already coaching her through each time she got up tonight. They said the bed was too high, and by the time I got there the three-inch pillow top was already off, and Grandpa had the sheets in the laundry.

By the time Mom and I walked and talked, she had talked to Uncle Brian. He took Grandpa to coffee to loosen him up with caffeine, and then he took notes as they talked. Grandpa said his best-case scenario is for he and Grandma to be able to move together to assisted living, but there's no availability. He agreed when Uncle Brian gave him numbers that assisted living—even with extra caregivers—would be the fiscally best option, too.

And that's when I stopped listening. Because there is availability. A woman gave her thirty-day notice this week. There is an open unit.

Mom and I tried to fight our mounting excitement. We don't know the technical results of the assessments. And we don't know if Grandpa will be as willing to go to assisted living when he finds out it is possible. We don't know a great deal.

It's another lesson in not getting too far ahead of ourselves. Too much is out of our hands . . . it's all out of our hands.

So I'll do what I can do. Tomorrow after work I'll go hang out with Grandma. And then the next day, and the next, and the next, for as many tomorrows as I can I will spend them with her wherever she is for however long we get.

Friday, March 28

For this season . . . That's how a friend described my day-to-day routine.

For this season. It's my reality. It won't always be, but for this season it is.

The words infused significance into what feels like an indefinite period that will linger on and on. But it won't. It will end. And this seasonal norm will be an isolated—though deeply meaningful—blip on my life's journey. This is the moment to be all in because the moments are numbered. My inability to see the end doesn't alter its approach.

It's the season to hold Grandma's hand and her memories. To pour out the love that has been poured so extravagantly into me.

Seasons are nebulous. In southern California, a date on the calendar doesn't always dictate what's outside the door. Nature works differently here: earthquake weather, El Niño, June gloom, fire season, Santa Ana winds.

Maybe that's why I struggle to identify the seasons of life as they happen. They don't follow predictable patterns or arrive on schedule neatly labeled. They come and they go . . . sometimes they overlap. They blow in with force or roll in like a fog bank. They're hot and dry, or they're mild and refreshing. They're part of a bigger system than an annual cyclical rhythm. And I never know how long they'll be drawn out or how quickly they'll pass.

So in an ongoing season of singleness I can make the most of being a daughter, a sister, an aunt. And my grandmother's granddaughter. Winds of change are swirling through our family. I can be present and responsive without needing to predict the shifting patterns or forecast what may—or may not—be heading toward us.

Yet whatever comes, it will be but a season. Longing for seasons gone by or hoping for seasons that may be to come doesn't change the season I find myself knee-deep in right now. It is how I live this moment of this season that counts.

For this season.

Monday, March 31

Friday was a day of unbelievable highs and unexpected lows. Grandma is NOT going back to skilled nursing on April 1! The results from the assessment came back, and Lori and others decided she isn't a good candidate. She's too healthy and too strong.

Uncle Brian broke the news to Grandpa that he's getting his best-case scenario. An apartment is opening in assisted living, and until then Grandma is cleared to stay in independent living with him and 24-hour caregivers.

It's what I wanted all along, but I'd done my best to bury the faint hope of its possibility. Elation. Unmitigated joy. Grandma doesn't have to move. She doesn't have to be in an unfamiliar room. She doesn't have to spend her days alternating between a bed and a wheelchair. She doesn't have to fret about the people passing her door so quickly all she can see is *"their tails as they go by."* She doesn't have to wait for help she won't ask for to get to the bathroom. She can sit in her own chair, eat at her own table, look at her own flowers out her own sliding door, sleep in her own bed, walk when she wants to walk.

And while celebrating another miracle in Grandma's life, her great-grandson was rushed to the hospital. Little, two-month old Aaron was struggling to breathe. Unlike his great-grandma he tested negative for pneumonia, but a virus was straining his body's ability to breathe.

Dancing on the doorstep of joy for Grandma and kneeling on the precipice of uncertainty for Aaron. Delight and despair hand-in-hand.

Tuesday, April 15

Unbelievable. That's the word everyone keeps saying.

It is unbelievable how far Grandma has come. It is unbelievable how well she is doing.

April 1 came and went. She's still home. And that's where she's staying. The directors have agreed to let both Grandpa and Grandma remain in independent living indefinitely. The caregivers have been cut back to just 7 a.m. to 7 p.m. Grandpa moved from sleeping in the La-Z-Boy to sharing a bed with Grandma. They added an adjustable rail to her side of the bed to help remind her not to get up unassisted during the night. And she's doing fine.

Uncle Brian and I were sharing April Fools' memories from years past. And then he said, "Mom, I saw Bill Ramm the other day."

"Oh, Bill."

"He still remembers you teaching Pam how to fill his medicine cabinet with ping pong balls."

"I did do that! Oh, goodness, I'd forgotten." Her shoulders bobbed and dipped as she laughed softly at one of her many pranks.

It made me think of the very first time she was ever at Daryl and Doreen's house—they were a young couple brand new to the church—Doreen had been folding laundry, so Grandma taped the fly shut on a pair of Daryl's boxers. Just because.

On Monday the 7th, Mom and I arrived after work with anniversary gifts to celebrate Grandpa and Grandma's fifty-second anniversary. Mom placed the stargazer lily plant on the patio as Grandma oohed and aahed over Dad's artwork on their envelope. I slid the graham cracker pie—her mother's recipe—into the fridge. And then Mom, Grandpa, April and I all crowded around Grandma's chair and watched the slideshow from their fiftieth anniversary again. We laughed and reminisced about each picture and accompanying memory. And then Grandpa excused himself to go to the dining hall for dinner. Grandma is still eating her pureed diet in their apartment.

Friday was the first visit from the physical therapist. Grandpa told me about it while Grandma rolled her eyes.

"He gave her all kinds of exercises to do every day," he said.

"That's great!"

Grandma looked unconvinced.

"You made me lay down on the floor and do all of mine every morning," Grandpa reminded her.

"That was for your health."

"I think this is for your health, too." I pointed out.

Her skeptical gaze made me laugh.

"He had surgery."

"Well, yes, but this is to help you to be able to do more without help, right? Don't you want that?"

She changed the subject.

Last Saturday, April 12, Uncle Brian and Aunt Jill picked Grandpa and Grandma up and brought them to Kevin and Wendy's house—the house on Birchleaf Drive where Grandpa and Grandma lived for forty-six years. Before Grandma even made it up the walk she was remarking on how good it felt to be there, how much she loved that house, what fond memories it held, how it was her favorite place she had ever lived. And then, because we weren't going to puree her food, Grandma ate pasta with chicken and half a slice of pizza. Aunt Jill and Dad cut everything up into small bites for her, but I don't think it would have mattered. She was so happy to be chewing food again. She ate an entire piece of cake with strawberries for dessert. Hopefully she'll do well on her barium swallow test this Thursday and be cleared to eat whatever she wants, whenever she wants.

After Kayla finished opening her presents, Kevin told her to go sit with Grandpa. She climbed up onto her great-grandpa's lap, still swinging the "tails" on her new robe she'd promptly put on after opening it. I carried Aaron over to Grandma and nestled all 13 pounds 6 ounces of him into her arms. And then the cameras started. After Kayla climbed down and returned to her Legos, Grandma kept holding Aaron murmuring about how perfect he was.

The next morning she went to church for the first time since December. She had to take her walker and caregiver . . . rather, she chose to take her caregiver to ensure *she* heard the message, too. And by Sunday afternoon she'd begun leaving her walker at the door when she re-entered the apartment. Both my grandparents seem to think walking assistance is for public walking only. In the apartment walkers and canes need not be used.

As Mom and I walked through the lobby yesterday, I caught a glimpse of Grandma and April sitting out in the courtyard, so we headed out to join them. She twisted in her chair and squinted in to the sun to see us as we walked up from behind her. She looked so beautiful in her navy slacks, yellow and white vertically striped shirt with the turquoise butterfly pattern on the cuffs and turquoise flower earrings. Sitting in the afternoon sun next to the fountain, she looked like a queen holding court.

We chatted about Kayla's fourth birthday party on Saturday and Amy's party we'll combine with Easter this coming Sunday.

Then Jeff the chef came out and joined us. He held her hand and joked with her. He told her how she was his favorite resident. And he'd even tolerate that big guy who was usually with her because he loved her so much. She soaked it all up, motioning for him to continue showering her with compliments. After Jeff left to help Dr. Pierre, we made our way back to their apartment and said hello and goodbye to Grandpa.

I leaned over to kiss Grandma goodbye.

"I won't be here tomorrow, but I'll see you on Wednesday."

"You aren't coming?"

"Not tomorrow, but I'll see you in less than 48 hours."

"I'll try to make it. I don't know if I can go that long without you."

Her eyebrows danced as she smiled at me.

"I love you."

"I love you, Honey."

Thursday, April 17

I wonder how many people are praying for Grandma. I know it's a lot. People I've almost forgotten I asked to pray stop me at church or email me at work—people who've never even met her—to check on how she's doing. Friends who don't pray text and call to remind me they're thinking of her. And those are my circles. What about Mom's and Uncle Brian's circles? What about my brothers' and cousins' circles? Or the prayer lists of multiple churches? She still gets cards from people we don't recognize who somehow heard she was ill and love her so much they wanted to contact her. Her life has touched that many people . . . and then more.

I watch her with her caregivers. Young women who have known her a month or less, who have names she can't remember, but who have been folded into the fabric of our family nonetheless. These women loved her at hello and try to do most of their job surreptitiously to avoid her fretting that they're spoiling her and she should be doing more so they don't have to. They seem to marvel at how many people come so regularly to see her, but then they get to know her more, and it becomes less surprising.

A few months ago, when Grandma was so ready to go home to be with her Lord, we kept reminding her she couldn't go until she had fulfilled her purpose here. And we believed it, in theory. But we didn't grasp the breadth of her purpose. I didn't understand the deep and lasting impact she makes on people in the briefest of encounters. In three months, she's touched so many people she wouldn't have come in contact with if she hadn't been sick. And she doesn't even know she's doing it. Her fingerprints cover so many lives.

And I don't know how many more days and weeks and months we may have. I know her recovery has exceeded all expectations and dreams. But I don't think it's about us. I think our increased time with her has been an exceptionally rich byproduct of her continuing to live her remarkable life as only she can and reach people only she can reach. And I'm okay with that.

I'm learning to watch and be present and savor these moments, and I'm stunned on an almost minute-by-minute basis at how the prayers are answered. Not because they're answered in what I presume to be the affirmative—that generally isn't happening. It's like we're praying for miracles, but we're praying for miracles we can imagine, and God can't be limited by our stunted imaginations. Even if the outcome is exactly what I wanted (like Grandma being able to stay at home), the way it happens, the route He takes, the methods He uses, the timing—all of it—transpires in a manner I couldn't have mapped out in advance if I'd tried.

Yesterday we went to the memorial service for Aunt Pat. Dad, Mom, Aunt Jill, Uncle Brian and I sat in the row in front of April, Grandma and Grandpa. We watched the slideshow of the Aunt Pat we remember and the Aunt Pat we never knew. We sang the songs layered in meaning and memory. We listened to the stories. We laughed. We teared up. We nodded. We celebrated and sighed and looked forward to the day we'll be together again.

There were lots of hugs and surprises at who was there—the connections cross so beautifully in this great, big family—and, of course, there was food. I'm not sure if I was more excited to see Grandma hugging friends she hadn't seen in years or seeing her make short work of her ham and cheese sandwich, pasta salad and cookies. I wish I'd thought to record it as evidence of her mastication skills to present to the doctors at her barium swallow test today.

It's a reminder to remember. Three months into a journey I didn't want to take I couldn't be more grateful for each moment of it, even the hard ones. Yet I'm already forgetting. I'm forgetting the pain and frustration and helplessness, and I'm forgetting the joy and amazement and peace.

Sunday, April 27

A speech pathologist named Frances came to evaluate Grandma's swallowing.

First she asked Grandma some questions. "How long have you been married?"

"Hmmm, maybe about forty-five years?"

"Well, Mom, Brian is more than fifty now," Mom coached.

Grandma looked around at our faces.

"On April 7th we celebrated our fifty-second anniversary," Grandpa said.

Frances oohed and aahed appropriately. Then she asked

Grandma about the key to a long-lasting marriage, but Grandma got a little turned around in her response. Frances asked Grandpa.

"Well, when we got married, we didn't really go to church. But then a friend invited Joanne, and she went. And so then we went. And our family is built around God. We all serve our Lord as best we can, and He's the most important part. We have a great family."

Frances turned back to Grandma. "And how old are you, Maxine?"

Grandma thought for a while. *"I'm getting up there . . . seventy?"*

"Next month we're going to celebrate your ninetieth birthday," I offered.

Grandma looked dismayed.

Frances showed us all a video of how the swallowing process is supposed to work, and some of the issues that can arise as people age and the process doesn't work quite so seamlessly. Then she explained how easy it can be for someone who isn't swallowing properly to aspirate food into the lungs but fail to have the normal coughing response most people have if food goes down the wrong way. And when that happens, pneumonia can develop.

The paranoia over Grandma's swallowing finally made sense. As Mom, Dad and I left Frances prepared to have lunch with Grandma to assess her chewing and swallowing.

Beginning of May

Meals in the dining hall are now medically approved, though she's actually been going for a couple weeks. And as each piece of the old routine slips back into place Grandma seems quicker and sharper. She never complained, but she struggled to find her way in the abnormality of the past few months. She doesn't remember being in the hospital or rehab or skilled nursing. Most days I'm not sure she knows who the caregivers are or why they are there. But she knows it hasn't always been this way.

She has developed coping mechanisms. She doesn't recognize people or track conversations, but instead of getting frustrated or questioning she watches and listens until a name is supplied or an answer is offered. She waits and trusts she'll understand. And then she does. Her patience and faith is amazing.

Mom and I were walking and talking about Grandma late one afternoon. As we rounded a corner she said, "There's something I should tell you. I probably should have told you a long time ago. I just never knew how. I mean, I didn't want you to think less of Grandma. Not that you would. It's just, I don't know."

"I know about Grandma's first husband," I replied.

"You do?!?"

"Yes. She told me when I was trying to make a family tree right before or right after our Michigan trip."

"Do your brothers know?"

"I have no idea. I never talked to anyone about it. But she brought him up again a few weeks ago when I was asking her something about your dad, and her answer didn't make any sense. Turns out she was talking about him, but neither of us could remember his name."

"Buzz something . . . Mc-something," Mom said.

"Buzz. That's funny I was thinking 'Bud,' but I was pretty sure that was wrong. Not too far off. I have it written down somewhere with my Michigan stuff. How long were they married?"

"Not very long. A year or two?"

"Is that how she came out here?" I asked.

"I really don't remember the details. I know when it ended she wrote a letter to his parents. That was the hardest part for her. She really loved his parents and in the letter she told them they had been the best part of the marriage."

Tuesday, May 13

Yesterday a chat on my work email popped up from Mom: "Please call me at 5263."

In the split second it took to grab my phone and punch in her extension I've known by heart for fifteen years thoughts raced through my mind:

- Grandma.
- It's serious if she can't remember my extension.
- It's really serious if she's telling me her extension.
- Stay calm.
- I'm supposed to leave for Israel in six days.
- Grandma first.

Her voice was flat when she answered. Grandpa called. Grandma was on her way to the emergency room. Possibly a stroke. Mom was going to go pick Grandpa up and take him. She'd come back for me later since it was a carpool day. Everything seemed to be okay.

"I want to go."

"I don't think you need to."

"I want to. I just need a minute to shut stuff down."

I called my supervisor and told him I was heading to the hospital but I'd take my computer and either work from there or finish later from home.

"Whatever you need to do. Go. Family first."

The best words I could have heard right then.

Only one person was allowed to be back with Grandma while they were running tests, so Grandpa asked Mom to go. He and I commandeered a corner of the emergency waiting room. He pulled out a book, and I pulled out my laptop. Having work to do was a good distraction from the waiting.

Mom came out with an update. Grandma was doing well. The slurred speech was mostly gone. She slept through the ultrasound of her carotid artery, and as the technician said, "She has beautiful anatomy."

Aunt Jill arrived.

Eventually the doctors decided they'd like to keep her overnight for further observation.

Both of her parents died after having strokes. Care was much different in the 1950s, but the complications eventually took them both. Less than a year apart. She was thirty-two when her dad died, and thirty-three when her mom died. I don't know if that went through Grandma's mind or not. It went through mine.

At the age I am now, she'd lost both her parents, one sister, been through a divorce, was living and raising her five-year old daughter thousands of miles from her family and was in a floundering marriage to an alcoholic who was on his last professional leg.

Her life when strokes rocked her parents' lives—and her own—was far different than mine as I sat and waited to hear the prognosis following her stroke.

Later last night Mom and Dad and I visited her in her hospital room, she had no idea where she was or why the nice lady wouldn't let her leave a note for Grandpa so he wouldn't worry about her. As soon as she's out of her home and routine, the confusion gets worse. She wanted to brush her teeth—some things stay the same.

When it was time for us to go she wanted to go with us.

And yet there were no long-term affects of the stroke beyond increased fatigue. Her speech returned to normal within five hours. She was tired and a bit weaker, but she was herself.

In fact, she diagnosed herself. As Grandpa was preparing her plate in the dining hall and she was chatting with the other couple at their table, she noticed her mouth felt funny. The corner was drooping. And she sounded funny. When Grandpa got back, she leaned over and told him, "I think I'm having a stroke."

Amazing.

Just days before the stroke, Grandpa had cancelled the twelve-hour-a-day caregivers. After the stroke they were back. But soon the schedule shifted to caregiving only from 7 a.m. to noon to help with showering, hair, makeup and physical therapy-prescribed exercises. The afternoons and evenings were back to long-lost normal. And Grandma couldn't be happier.

Saturday, May 17

I walked in the door today.

"How was your trip?"

"I haven't gone yet. I leave tomorrow," I said as I kissed Grandma.

Her face fell. *"Oh."*

"I know I wasn't here yesterday, but I don't leave until tomorrow. As soon as I get back, I'll come see you."

"*Okay.*"

"You'll be my first stop, I promise."

"*Okay.*"

"And next weekend Jon and Angela and Norah will be down to see you. They're coming to celebrate your birthday with you."

"*And you?*"

"Well, I won't be here for the party. I'll still be in Israel. But you and I will celebrate when I get back. We'll make your birthday last even longer."

Sunday, May 18—somewhere over Europe

It feels strange to be on a plane heading away from my family. It feels even stranger to be unplugging for ten days.

I left an emergency contact number. Mom knows how to get a message to me. If anything happens with Grandma, I want to know the very first second I can.

But I know me. If I have the ability to be plugged in, I'll be searching for Internet connections every chance I get even when the time difference dictates they'll all be asleep at home. So I brought nothing with me to tempt me to get online. No phone, no computer, no tablet. Fully unplugged.

This is a trip I need to be present for—I need to be in the moment taking in all I can, not straddling roles and half-listening to two sides of the globe at once.

Maybe it'll be just another trip. But I don't think so. It's Israel. I'm finally going to have a physical setting, a mental image, for the book I know better than any other. Ten days of digging into the context and culture and all the things I can't even imagine—fleshing out thin spots in my faith . . . I hope.

Monday, May 26

Grandma turned ninety today. All day I kept wondering if I should try to borrow a phone and call her tonight. But she'll have everyone else with her today, and if she doesn't notice I'm not there, would it make it worse to be reminded?

Grandma turned ninety as I slipped back to the first century and beyond. The Mount of Olives, Bethlehem, the Western Wall—even deep below the current city but still thirty feet above where Jesus walked—and then splashing through the cold, clear water in Hezekiah's Tunnel. Tracing the water from the Spring of Gihon to the Pool of Siloam, fingers trailing along the walls inches wider than my shoulders. Emerging from underground in the late afternoon to hike back up the hill to Jerusalem. We made our way through the wall and wove through the city.

A city with such history and such presence.

In a little more than a day I'll be flying home. I need to leave as much of me here as possible, so I have room to take as much of here home as possible.

Wednesday, May 28

I landed at LAX at 6:35 a.m. My feet and legs swelled up to disturbing proportions on the fifteen-and-a-half hour flight, so after getting a shower and unpacking I bought compression socks.

I spent an hour with my compressed legs elevated over my heart, and when I couldn't take it any more I headed over to see Grandma and Grandpa. I hadn't been apart from her for more than two days since she got sick, and now it'd been ten days.

Opening the door and seeing her smile set my restless heart at ease.

Wednesday, June 11

As we chatted Grandma asked if I had any more trips planned. It was one of the first times since I got back she remembered I'd been back. For days I was greeted and then asked about my trip. We would go through it all as though I'd come straight from the airport that day.

"No, nothing else planned right now. I should probably put in some time in the office. Maybe next month I'll go up and see Jon and Angela and Norah for a weekend."

"That'd be nice . . . I wish you and I could go away for a few days . . . I just get so tired these days."

"That would be fun. You know there's nothing wrong with taking a nap now and then."

"I just think about Mom and Dad and how they never took naps. They worked from morning 'til night."

"You worked from morning to night for a lot of years, too. I think once you hit the big nine-oh you're allowed to take a nap. And you made it to ninety, so you can nap now."

She just humphed at me but smiled.

"When Grandpa said he had a doctor's appointment I asked if I would go along and he said, 'oh, no,' and I thought 'oh, good.' I thought I'd be alone and could just lie down. Then he said this morning Donna was going to come sit with me, and I thought, 'oh, crud! Now I can't lie down.'"

But she doesn't view me coming to sit with her the same. I don't think it occurs to her I might be sitting her as well. It's just me coming to be with her.

Right when I walked in Donna showed me where the check was and told me Grandma had an appointment to get her nails done at 3:45. After Donna left, I asked Grandma where the beauty shop was because the only one I knew was over by skilled nursing, and I couldn't imagine her having to walk that far. She had no idea. So when it was time to go, we stopped by the front desk and I asked Elaine. Good thing, we never would have found it on our own. As it was I had to leave her rifling for a Kleenex while I double-checked the hall we'd passed to see if it was the right one.

As we passed the Admin door Jeff, the chef, was inside but leaning on the glass door. Grandma paused and let go of her walker, then she looked at me, *"I was just going to give that a pull, but I guess I better not."*

"Hmm, probably better not to start something you can't finish."

She grinned—no loss of humor there—and we continued along.

As we waited for Carmen to finish with her earlier client, Grandma looked at the check. *"Did he put the tip on?"*

"I'm sure he did. He filled it all out."

"But the tip?"

"I'm not sure how much it costs, but I'm sure he included a tip. Grandpa wouldn't skip a tip."

Grandma chuckled and then flipped up the seat on her walker and murmured something about maybe she had it.

"Look at all that! A sweater, a whole box of Kleenex, a purse."

"I don't have a purse."

I pulled out a purse.

"Whose is that?"

"It's yours. Look here's Kleenex and more Kleenex—"

"Sounds like mine."

"A little low on cash though, I only found a penny."

"Then it must be mine."

She continued fidgeting with the check as I reloaded the basket. "I have cash if he forgot."

"Okay."

As soon as Grandma sat down and put her feet in the water, she was asleep. Carmen trimmed and filed. Grandma only wakened when her feet were gently raised and lowered from the water. I guess she was as tired as she admitted in the apartment.

Gwen, the hairdresser, returned soon. She and Grandma started chatting. I knew I needed to leave, but I wasn't sure if Grandma would be able to find her way back to the apartment on her own.

"Grandma, I need to get going, but Grandpa is in your apartment," I trailed off as I looked toward Gwen.

"Well, we'll just have to go see him when you're done," Gwen told her as she winked at me.

Thursday, June 26

I'm a little homesick today. Homesick for a place that's never been home. Not physically at least.

I went—almost on a whim—for eight and a half days, but it was something more than another trip. It reached down inside me and grabbed this and grabbed that and threaded them together in the most unexpected way.

I went with no expectations. I went because why not go.

And going changed me.

There was no beam of light from heaven or profound moment of revelation. I didn't hear God's audible voice. It wasn't any thing at all. It was one seemingly small moment after another.

It was being in a cistern and understanding the terror Joseph must have felt.

It was standing on a hilltop—descending to the valley floor and picking smooth stones out of a riverbed—and realizing the enormity of David's illogical courage. His boldness could have been the end of his entire nation, if he failed. And every shred of reason said he would fail.

It was standing in an underground columbarium and glimpsing a fraction of the volume of doves whose lives were destined for a sacrificial system that could never atone for people's sins.

It was watching shepherds tend sheep in the middle of a desert.

It was riding on a camel whose ingeniously designed feet allow it to traverse inhospitable land.

It was seeing an oasis in the middle of a desert canyon.

It was being in the water of the Dead Sea and then being in the living water of the Jordan River and the Mediterranean Sea.

It was standing in the blazing heat on top of Masada and understanding what a stronghold is. What a refuge is. What a rock is.

It was looking into the caves of Ein Gedi and beginning to grasp the juxtaposition of fleeing to a source of life in a dead land.

It was driving through valleys and traversing hills that made the life-and-death reality of safe passage and control of trade routes become more than historical trivia.

It was looking at a sycamore tree and realizing the desperation an outcast felt that led him to seek just a glimpse of Jesus with no expectation of a result.

It was seeing the ruins of modest basalt-rock villages and magnificent Greco-Roman cities that made real the strength of people living in a world with none of the conveniences I deem necessary.

It was sitting on Mt. Carmel overlooking the Jezreel Valley—the breadbasket of a nation—and imagining the devastation of three years without rain and the confidence of Elijah to not only believe God would answer but to taunt his opponents and then stack the deck against himself.

It was walking the ruined streets of Chorazin and Capernaum, slipping into the synagogues and feeling the hope they pegged on just trying harder to keep the unkeepable law while missing the Hope who was fulfilling the law in their midst.

It was standing on the shores of the Sea of Galilee and wondering how vindicated those fishermen who'd washed out of the religious education system felt when a rabbi chose them.

It was sitting on a rock outcropping atop Mt. Arbel looking over the lake and feeling the sadness of a people still searching for a savior in a place He most likely came to pray for them.

It was the wind whipping against me on a boat in the middle of the lake, watching the waves and wondering if I could ever have the faith Peter had—if only for seconds—that propelled his feet onto the water.

It was sharing a Shabbat dinner to the sound of the lake lapping the shore.

It was standing on the mosaic-ed floor of Herod's palace jutting into the Mediterranean and being awed by the audacity and dismayed by the egotism.

It was staring across the Kidron Valley at the Temple Mount wondering where Jesus found the strength to volunteer to take on the abuse of my sins, so I might know the freedom He designed me for.

It was hiking up to Jerusalem and listening in my mind to the throngs reciting the Psalms of Ascent as they made their pilgrimage.

It was running my fingers along the cornerstone and understanding no place is undefeatable, but I have a Cornerstone that will never be thrown down.

It was weaving my way through crowded city streets and imagining the voices hurling scorn on the One who knew them and loved them anyway.

It was singing with one voice in chapels of little consequence other than marking the places the One to whom we sing once stood.

It was eating the very foods God promised His people He would provide for them in the land He promised to provide.

It was constructing context and a setting for the book I've read in a vacuum.

It was being fully present in a place I knew only in theory.

And today I'm homesick for it.

I'm homesick for the grace and compassion the land stirred in my soul when I stood and saw and felt the magnitude of the ripples spreading through time from one small point on a map.

Friday, July 11

Yesterday was Grandpa's angiogram, which then included an angioplasty to clear one artery with a seventy percent obstruction.

Mom picked Grandpa and Grandma up and took them to the hospital. There were a couple hours to wait until his scheduled 3:30 start time. I got off work early and headed to the hospital to wait with them.

I could tell when I walked into the radiology waiting room that Grandma was tired. She held my hand as she nodded off to the sound of the TV—I don't think she knew where we were or why.

Routine is Grandma's friend, and there is nothing routine about hospitals. When Jessica arrived shortly before four o'clock we suggested she take Grandma home and have dinner with her. Grandma didn't protest. While Jess went to pull her car around to the closest entrance, I began walking with Grandma.

"She doesn't need to get the car. I can walk."

"The parking structure is a long way. You could probably walk home in the time it would take to get there. But it's no trouble for Jess to come pick you up."

"I could walk home."

"I have no doubt."

"Where are we heading?"

"All the way down this hall . . . then see that brown wall up there? We're going to turn, and then we should be almost there."

We made our way down the hall with Grandma greeting and smiling at each person who passed us. As we made the turn toward the south waiting room Grandma asked, *"Are we almost there?"*

"Yep, just through those doors, and we'll be outside."

"Oh, good."

We walked outside and I scanned to see if there was somewhere to sit.

"Grandma, would you like to sit in the shade or would it feel better to sit in the sun?"

She looked back and forth and then looked at me.

"How about right here? Mostly shade but nice and warm. We'll see Jess when she pulls up."

"Jessica is picking us up?"

"She's picking you up. She's going to take you home, and then she'll stay and have dinner with you so the two of you can get a little time together."

"Oh."

"And then Mom will be over later, and she'll spend the night with you. Just like old times."

"Oh, good."

"And I'm working from home tomorrow, so I'll be over in the morning, too."

"This is nice."

Jess arrived, and we got Grandma settled into the front seat. After they drove off, I arrived back in the waiting room a few minutes before Grandpa's doctor came in with a report.

"He has the heart of a man in his fifties. It went great. One stent. He has nice big arteries, so we went in through the arm. He did great. They'll take him upstairs right now, and you can go see him. He should be good to go home in the morning."

And that's how it went. This morning I arrived to stay with Grandma and April while Mom headed to the hospital. Grandpa came home feeling great and with a clean bill of heart-related health.

Later this evening Mom said, "Do you know what my sweet mother said last night?"

"What?"

"We'd had such a fun evening chatting, and when we were getting ready for bed she said, *'Now, Honey, which side of the bed do you prefer?'* And I said, 'Oh, Mom, you sleep right here—' on her side '—and I'll sleep over here.' Can you believe that? Still thinking about others first."

"Sounds like Grandma."

Saturday, August 2

Before my trip to Israel I visited Grandma six or seven days a week. A few times I'd missed two days back to back. But after Israel I cut back to visiting three or four times a week most weeks. Sometimes more. Never less. It's not for lack of love—far from it—but it's hard to get off work at 4:00, get to their apartment at 4:25, then have them leave for dinner at 5:00 and spend another half an hour or more crawling through rush-hour traffic to get seven miles to home.

I'm an introvert. Without question. And the months of having very little quiet time and very little alone time started to take a toll. The pace of going from work to hospital—or rehab or skilled nursing or apartment—then often on to other evening activities for five months was a privilege, but it cost. And as summer started and Grandma's health was stable, I had to adjust.

And what a miracle that is. Grandma's health was stable. Even with a re-cracked rib and a couple falls, she was stable.

Doctors don't know what to make of her. They say things like amazing and beautiful as they look back and forth from test results to her. On paper she shouldn't be sitting in front of them. Her bronchial tubes are so scarred parts of her lungs aren't even getting oxygen. And yet she smiles and chats with them and has no complaint about her breathing.

Back in January the head pulmonologist, Dr. Chan, offered hope she might survive the pneumonia. But when I pushed him, he admitted we were most likely talking weeks to months. The look I received when I mentioned her ninetieth birthday in May was one closer to pity than possibility. And he may prove right on the months' front, but today is already August. We're less than a week from the seven-month mark of her being admitted to the hospital.

I never hoped for today. I never hoped as I sat by her bed that she would get her routine back. I wanted it. But it seemed too big to even dream. When she moved home, I was elated, but I didn't think she could keep improving. And after the stroke, I was so worried about setbacks and whether or not this would be the first of multiple strokes, I just assumed she'd peaked and would decline.

I've never been happier to be wrong. My faith is small. My imagination constrained by my reading of reality. My ability to dream rocked by fear of being disappointed. Aim low. It'll hurt less when I crash.

And yet as I've aimed low, God has aimed high. His love for Grandma—His love for me—is beyond extravagant. I wanted her dignity maintained. He wanted her courage honored.

Each day we draw closer to the day He will welcome her home. I'm not sure how much of these months she remembers or will remember in the near future, but I am quite sure the holes in her memory are not big enough to swallow the love and presence people have clamored to reflect back to her. Not one of us can repay how she has loved us, but it's been a privilege and a comfort for us to try. And I have to believe it's been a small foretaste for her of the Love that will envelop her one day soon.

Sunday, August 3

I arrived as church let out today. Grandma was walking with Cam. Grandpa was twenty feet behind. Grandma broke into a grin when she saw me just as Grandpa called out a greeting. She pushes her walker so far in front of her she's almost bent at a ninety-degree angle. It makes me nervous. But I don't say anything. The last thing she needs is her granddaughter telling her how to walk in front of her fellow residents.

We caught up on how we each slept last night, and I recounted how old the Nordell girls are now. Last night was Alli's seventh birthday party. Neither of us can be quite sure where the years have gone or how the girls could be so old.

When it was time for me to go, I gave Grandma a kiss and whispered, "I love you."

"I love you so much. You're so special to me."

"You're so special to me. I think I'm going to keep you, would that be all right?"

"Yes. Good thing the price is so low on the tag."

"Oh no—you're priceless."

She smiled at me as I squeezed her knee.

"I'll see you tomorrow."

"Love you, Honey."

As I drove home I started thinking about how poorly I've been sleeping. Lots of strange, troubling dreams. Is there a connection to writing? Or to not writing?

Since Grandma has been doing so well, I've stopped writing about her. I've hardly written at all the past few months. And I think it's significant.

Writing is my memory bank. I write to process, but I also write to remember. Once I've written it, I don't need to try so hard to hold onto it. I can let it go entirely because I know it's safe. I can get it back. I can feel it, smell it, hear it again. But when I fail to write it down I try to retain the memories and instead they swirl and mix and collide with the rest of life—trivial and important—and become jumbled and disheveled. Some disappear forever. I mine the fragments and get frustrated by the chaos and the effort of piecing back together what I thought I could never forget.

The gift of the written word is the space it frees up inside me. I can immerse myself in the moment because my hands are free. I'm no longer trying to cram the seconds between the cracks in the memories clutched in my fingers. I'm not searching for associations to hang the new minutes on if I've taken the time to capture the previous ones in words.

And when life is hard and the moments are thick with emotion and unknown, it's easier to stop and sit and pound them into a keyboard and out of my heart. It's almost effortless because I know I don't have the capacity to keep them roiling inside me—I have to get them out. But when life thins and the moments feel lighter and borderline predictable I forget how heavy they sit inside of me. I forget they accumulate and weigh on me in their unprocessed, unwritten state.

So there's no news today. We covered no new ground. We walked the deepest path of love. But some day I might not remember the feel of her slacks against my hand or how she looked me right in the eye as she whispered her reminder that I am loved and special. I might misplace the memory of the extraordinary bond we share. And so I play it over in my mind on the drive home and then find words to record it. There are moments I can stand to forget, but forgetting moments with her is unacceptable.

Thursday, August 7

I look down at our hands—fingers laced together—when did my hands become bigger than hers? I knew time and aging had reversed our heights. But our hands? I hadn't realized.

In these past seven months I've held these hands for minutes and hours and days. And somewhere as those seconds slid by our roles shifted from her hand being my security to mine being hers.

These hands—that into her sixties were strong enough to twist an apple in two—now hold mine with uncomplicated faith; confident they are safe. Just as my nieces reach for my hands to guide them across streets, Grandma reaches for me to guide her through the afternoon.

I feel each bone and tendon under her smooth, delicate skin. I look at her long, strong fingernails and see my own, right down to the curve of the thumbnail.

The stories her hands tell. Collecting eggs. Fumbling with buttons in the cold, upstairs bedroom of the farmhouse. Carrying wood for the stove in the one-room schoolhouse. Scooping pork chops out of the lard-filled crock in the cellar. Driving cars and trucks and road graders. Flying over the keys of typewriters and filling steno pads with shorthand. Applying leg makeup. Popping sticks of gum into her mouth. Writing thousands of letters and cards. Keeping a spotless house. Ironing each Oxford shirt and pair of slacks. Basting the candied yams. Slicing the apples for deep-dish apple pie. Frosting Grandma Borgman's Fudge Cake. Playing practical jokes. Caring for her children, grandchildren and great-grandchildren.

So much of the strength of these hands is gone. But none of the grace.

As I get up to leave, her hand doesn't release. Her right hand rests on my cheek as she kisses me goodbye. She thanks me for coming and tells me she loves me. She watches expectantly for me to step away. But she doesn't let go. Holding her gaze I reach down to uncurl her fingers from mine. I rest her left hand on the armrest and rub a small circle on the back of her hand as I step backwards toward the door.

I walk to the car still feeling the gentle pressure of her hand in mine.

Sunday, August 17

Friday night we packed five of the six birthdays from July and August into one party. It was loud and a bit disjointed—late arrivals, mild miscommunications. Uncle Brian arrived first with Grandpa and Grandma.

I sat on the edge of the couch next to Grandma. "You look tired."

"I am."

She patted my hand.

Kevin, Wendy, Kayla and Aaron arrived. Mom picked Aaron up from the family room floor and brought all nineteen pounds of his seven-month self over to Grandma.

"Would you like to hold your great-grandson?"

"Oh, yes."

Grandma pulled Aaron to her shoulder. While Aaron is her cuddliest great-grandchild, he's a busy boy who wants to keep an eye on everything going on around him. Somehow he seemed to grasp the situation, and he nestled against her for a few minutes before his squirminess took him back to his toys and big sister on the floor.

Hours later as we packed up the leftovers, little ones and older ones, Kevin said to Kayla, "Give Great-Grandma a love."

"I already did."

"Give her another one."

Kayla reached to hug her as Grandma cupped Kayla's face and rubbed her cheek.

What memories will Kayla have of her great-grandma? Will she understand the way she's shaped this family? Will Kayla ever know how much of her daddy's playfulness was encouraged by his grandma? Will she know how much she loved each of us?

This morning after church I met Mom and Dad at Grandpa and Grandma's apartment. They weren't back from church yet. When they arrived, Grandma was all smiles but looked weary. She sank into her chair.

"Did it take most of yesterday to recover from Friday night?" Mom asked.

"Oh, no."

"She rested most of the day. But we had a great time," Grandpa added.

"It was wonderful."

Conversation over.

Thursday, August 21

Yesterday after work Mom and I arrived at Grandpa and Grandma's to find Uncle Brian and Amy already there.

We sat in a big noisy circle talking over the baseball game on TV. Grandma was tired and when Uncle Brian and I reminded her she is more than allowed to take a nap she rolled her eyes. A few seconds later as Grandpa talked across her to Mom, she looked across the room at me and began telling me a story as though we were the only two present.

"One day when I was fourteen or maybe twelve . . . twelve or fourteen . . . I asked Mom if after dinner—is that what we called it? Not supper."

"Yes, you called lunch 'dinner.'"

"Well, one day I asked Mom if after dinner, if I did all the dishes, you know, all my chores, real fast if she and I could lay down and take a nap.

"And she said, 'Well, I guess we could do that, Sister.'

"Oh, I was so excited. When dinner was over I was cleaning the kitchen as fast as I could. And then I heard a car toot. And I saw the car pulling around the driveway to the back of the house, which meant it was someone we knew well.

"It was my Aunt Lulu and Uncle Pete. Any other time I would be thrilled to see them. But, oh, I wanted that nap!"

"And you didn't get it?"

"No, we never did get it."

I'm not sure if I heard that story growing up, but I've heard it at least a half dozen times in the past six months. Usually she told it just as she did today. Once or twice they had just lain down when the car pulled up. Either way it is the nap narrative ingrained in Grandma's memory, and any suggestion she take a real nap—on a bed instead of dozing in her chair—stirs it inside her.

Sunday, August 24

"Guess what I did yesterday?"

"What?"

"I went skydiving?"

"You went skydiving?" Grandpa asked.

"I did. I jumped out of a plane. Well, actually, I didn't jump out of a plane. I was strapped to a guy who jumped out of a plane. I was just along for the ride."

"How was it?"

"It was amazing—you would have loved it!"

"I think I would have."

"It was better than a roller coaster."

"I don't think they'd let you go at your age," Grandpa cautioned.

"But if they would, you'd love it."

I spent twenty minutes trying and failing to explain what it felt like to freefall at one hundred twenty miles an hour with views of Southern California from Big Bear to Catalina Island. Then coast and soar thousands of feet before landing softly on our feet. And as I talked, Grandma smiled a wistful smile. There are adventures left inside her.

Wednesday, August 27

"You know that's one thing. I've never been to an Angels game."

"You haven't been this year to an Angels game," Mom prompted.
Grandma looked at her bewildered.

"Remember the year Ed and I took you? Their home opener was
on your anniversary, and we took you. It was so cold. By the fifth
inning even you and Daddy were frozen. I'd been a popsicle the
whole time. We left it was so cold."

No memory of it.

The door closed behind us, and as we walked down the hall our
shoulders sagged.

"I'm losing her . . . down a dark tunnel," Mom's eyes glistened as
she pursed her lips. "She really didn't know she was having dinner
with Donna. And you know Daddy told her repeatedly. But she
seemed to know he was going to dinner with Mick. I just don't
understand."

I rubbed her back as we walked.

When I could find words, I said, "Six months ago I didn't think
we'd still have her now."

"That's true . . . I didn't either."

Sunday, August 31

"How about we take you all out for a burger?"

"Do you want to go out to eat Mom?"

"I just think we should take you out."

"Where would you like to go?" I asked.

"Oh, anywhere."

"But you'd like a burger?"

"It does sound good."

We figured out cars and details, and headed to Polly's Pies for
lunch. The restaurant was crowded and a little loud. Grandpa and
Dad carried most of the conversation. Mom tried to engage
Grandma, but she seemed a bit lost.

The rest of us were done, and Grandma had abandoned her

burger and was picking at her fries when she caught my eye and mouthed, *"I have to go to the bathroom."*

"Okay, Grandpa will let you out." I said, as I turned to Grandpa, "Grandma needs to use the bathroom."

She and I were on opposite sides of the long booth slid all the way in by the walls. Dad jumped up and let Mom out to go with Grandma. Grandpa swung his legs out and got up as Grandma scooted out of the seat.

After a few minutes, the waitress brought our pie packaged to take home. Then she brought the bill.

"Do you think Grandma was done eating?"

Grandpa looked at her plate. She'd finished over half of her teriyaki burger and a third of her fries. "She'll forget about it."

"I was just thinking maybe we should go pay and meet them up front, so she doesn't have to walk all the way back here."

And I did think that, but I also knew too much time was passing. As Grandpa and Dad headed to the counter, I poked my head into the restroom. "Mom? We'll be in the lobby, okay?"

Grandpa sat in the waiting area. Dad and I stood. Antsy. Too much time.

When the door opened, my suspicions were confirmed. Grandma's shirt was untucked—her shirt is never untucked. She is the picture of proper. Over her right shoulder Mom was motioning for me to get the car. I was already half-way to the door.

I pulled up in front of the restaurant as they came down the ramp. Dad got Grandma into the front seat as Mom and I put her walker in the back.

"I'm so sorry."

"You have nothing to be sorry for. Everything is just fine."

"No, no."

"It is. You're perfect."

She fidgeted with her right sleeve. It was rolled a few uneven rolls. The embarrassment and humiliation radiated from her face.

In two minutes we were pulling up in front of the retirement home. I reached over and unbuckled her seatbelt. "Wait right here. I'll be around with your wheels in a second."

I set her walker near her open door and reached for her arm. I placed my hand to avoid the fresh stain. I grasped her other hand and pulled as gently as I could to remind her she had to help get out of the car.

Mom was quietly asking Grandpa to please finish getting her cleaned up and into fresh clothes as soon as possible. I rested my hand on her hunched back and leaned in for a kiss. I waited until she met my gaze. "I love you, my sweet grandma."

"I'm not sweet at all."

"You are. You are the sweetest."

Head down she made her way to the door.

I can only pray this will be one of the moments she forgets. But I know these are the very ones she remembers. She remembers the moments she's ashamed of—the ones she thinks make her less, the ones she can't control. And there is nothing I can do to rewrite the story she tells herself.

Sunday, October 12

Grandpa says the cough started on Thursday. I heard it last Sunday. At the time she dismissed it as a tickle. And were it anyone else, I'd have believed it, but it was still tickling on Monday and Wednesday.

It sounds innocent. So quiet and dry. But that's how it starts. And for someone whose lungs are as compromised as hers are, innocuous becomes pneumonia in hours, not days.

Last night the walk back from the dining hall left her winded. Grandpa called the nurse. Her oxygen levels were a robust ninety-eight, and she didn't cough once. But her temperature was 98.8°F— which sounds good except her normal is in the 97° range.

"How do you feel today?"

"All right."

"What does 'all right' mean?"

She motions toward the sliding door. *"I'm not going to go out and run laps."*

"Oh, you're not?" I laugh. "Neither am I."

She smiles and pats my hand. Subject closed.

I look beyond her to Grandpa. "Still probably a good idea to go see the doctor." They ignore me.

I forgot how delicate status quo is. I'd been lulled into a new normal of not worrying with each goodbye that it may be the last. But that cough . . . her fragile lungs have neither the elasticity nor the strength to wage this war again.

Several times she tried to tell a story, but I couldn't follow. She trailed off looking for words to restore sense to the narrative. I held her hand and heard Uncle Brian's voice in my head saying that last week she'd told him she'd gone to look for her parents, but she wasn't sure if they were still living given her own age. She didn't find them before Grandpa found her, but she couldn't figure out how he knew where she was. None of it seems likely, but she believes it, and how do we honor her memory as it fades? How do we buoy her dignity as she fights to make sense of an increasingly unfamiliar life?

I lean over to kiss her goodbye.

"I'll see you tomorrow. I love you."

"I love you . . . with all my heart."

My breath catches in my throat. She didn't follow our script. But I meet her eyes and whisper back, "I love *you* with all my heart."

Monday, October 13

When Mom and I walked in the door after work Grandpa was in his chair yelling into his cell phone. Grandma's chair was empty. I veered for the bedroom and on toward the bathroom. One-track mind: find Grandma.

Grandma and I walked out from the bathroom, and we all made our way to our positions. Grandma in her chair, I sat on the seat of her walker next to her, Mom pulled the other chair closer to hear over Grandpa's conversation with Uncle Brian on the phone. Grandma lifted her left hand and waited—I grabbed it with both of mine and didn't let go until we had to leave.

Even as I heard fragmented comments about Grandma's doctor's appointment, I wasn't sure what the result was, so I asked her about it.

She denied having seen a doctor but tapped her jaw and said something about Grandpa going to the dentist though she didn't go, and she didn't know why because her tooth ached.

I tried to keep a neutral face and fill in the words as she searched for them, but I failed. As she looked at me she knew it wasn't making sense and neither of us could find the words she thought she needed. She changed the subject.

But everything in me was screaming. Not five hours before she'd been in a doctor's office. He'd spent forty-five minutes with her. And she had no memory of it at all. Even when Mom prompted her with details, not a flicker of recognition crossed her face. Her days are slipping away from her faster and faster.

Grandpa hung up his phone and gave us the rundown: no fever, no cough (as she sat beside me and coughed), lungs sounded good, but her heart murmur—that pesky valve—sounded much worse. Hearts are not supposed to whoosh. Her heart is whooshing. She starts new medications tomorrow. She has a CT scan of her lungs on Thursday. Next week an echocardiogram to check on the valve. And she needs to see an infectious disease specialist. Maybe he can get to the bottom of this mysterious lung ailment that has eluded doctors for years.

She listened. She said nothing. Did she know we were talking about her? She waited for him to finish, and then she looked back and forth between Mom and me.

"It means so much that you come so often to see us. We know you're so busy, and you come so faithfully."

"There's nowhere I'd rather be."

"Well . . ."

It's true. There's nowhere I'd rather be.

Tears slipped out as I emailed a friend tonight with the update. How can I be so selfish? I'm not ready to say goodbye. I can't do it. I can't face life without my grandma. But the thought of her suffering . . . the look of bewilderment on her face when she realizes neither of us understand what she's saying . . . it knocks the breath out of me. The sound of her coughing and fighting to breathe. I'd do anything to avoid that.

And I beg for both. I beg to keep her, and I beg for her to know no pain. I cannot have both. But I plead anyway. I don't know what else to do.

Thursday, October 16

Time is slipping and sliding and racing through Grandma's fingers. What must it be like to retain the language of time but be unable to hang meaning from the words?

Perhaps it's why she is quieter now. Harder to engage. Eyes wandering to the sliding glass door more often as though the view might anchor her and bring welcome context to the confusing repetition of minutes.

As her gaze roamed to the door yesterday, I mentioned the weather. It's starting to feel like fall. At least in the evenings. But does that connect? I can almost see the years melt away and watch her struggle to reconcile the fall out the window—the one that is sunny and warm with trees still coated in green—with the fall of her childhood where the fields were barren, the trees shed their leaves and the air bit into exposed skin.

I couldn't help it; I needed to hear her voice. What was winter like on the farm? What did the men do when the fields were covered in snow?

She straightened in her chair and squeezed my hand a little tighter. We were in Michigan again. Not so much in winter. Not so much with the men repairing equipment and looking after the maintenance work that was so hard to do when crops and livestock and warm, daylight hours kept them running. But Michigan nonetheless. For twenty minutes her words flowed. The words she knew she wanted when she wanted them. She grabbed them and wove them without pause, only looping back to one thread four times, tightly knotting her story with how wonderful her brothers were to take her to the dances at the Grange Hall—how she was the envy of her friends whose own brothers didn't pay attention to them.

Bliss.

I had to interject. I had to leave. The clarity in her eyes clouded over even as she thanked me for coming and asked where I was going. The conversation when I'd arrived already beyond her recall. So I told her again, and kissed her goodbye and wiggled my fingers just a bit to prompt her own fingers to release.

I turned at the door for one last goodbye, one last "I love you." Her eyes were still on me, hand in the air, waiting to see if I was arriving or leaving.

Thursday, November 20

Grandma and Grandpa missed Bethany's wedding on Sunday. Grandma's low-grade fever and cough were back. Grandpa was disappointed. Age does not diminish his propensity to go stir crazy. He'd been looking forward to this outing for months. Calendars have lost their meaning for Grandma. She didn't remember the wedding was coming or that she missed it.

Yesterday as I held her hand Mom handed her a program from the wedding.

"I thought you might want to see the program from Bethany and Christian's wedding."

"Oh, yes."

Grandma read every word and oohed and aahed over the picture of the two of them on the back.

When she looked up, Mom said, "And we got some exciting news. Naomi—Dawn and Lewis' younger daughter—and her husband are expecting their first child in June."

"Who?"

"Dawn—Aunt Jackie's daughter? Aunt Jackie had two daughters, Denise and Dawn. The second daughter, Dawn, is married to Lewis—Kevin works for Lewis. Dawn and Lewis have two daughters, Krissy who is—"

"A little bit younger than me."

"—and Naomi. Naomi and Jason are expecting their first baby."

Grandma's head dipped in the slightest of nods, yet her expression betrayed her inability to place a single name or relationship Mom mentioned. And while these are Hartmann relatives, Grandma has known them for decades. Aunt Jackie's been gone for over twenty years, but she and Grandma were friends for thirty years.

When it was time to leave I leaned in for my kiss. "I love you."

"I love you. You're so precious."

I rested my forehead against her soft curls.

"I'll see you soon."

Mom called Jon last night with an update on Grandma. The fever seems to be gone. Her lungs are clear, but oxygen has been ordered as she is breathing too rapidly. Then Mom recounted the exchange about the wedding. Her voice quavered and I could hear the tears forming as she said, "She's slipping further away from me."

Tuesday, November 25

I reached for my recipe book—the one my sister-in-law created before I moved to Las Vegas. It holds one-hundred-one hand-written recipes from people who love me. Some with illustrations.

Recipes seventeen through twenty-one are from Grandma: Fudge Cake, Kookie Brittle, Dinner-in-a-dish, Sweet Kosher Pickles and Candied Yams. At the bottom of each page, she added a note.

This morning I needed the pickle recipe. I double-checked ingredients and made my list. Thanksgiving is coming, and it demands a relish tray of Grandma's pickles. Grandpa and I can finish the whole tray—maybe the jar—ourselves. A trip to Grandma's always meant a pickle or eight. And I can't count the number of birthdays or Christmases I received a jar of pickles just for me. Today my eyes drifted past the recipe to the note: *"To my pickle eater—this recipe came from a friend of Grandma Weinz and she was a Home Ec. teacher."*

Then my eyes settled on the Candied Yams recipe. I've never made them myself. Maybe because of the note: *"Kristen—this may be 'testy' a time or two around but you will do well. Aunt Verlyn (my sis) gave this recipe to me and we agree—Thanksgiving dinner wouldn't be the same w/o it."*

No, no it would not. Thanksgiving. It's the day I can't put into words. My favorite holiday. My favorite meal. My favorite people. It's thick with tradition and layered in memories. Like Grandma. Try as I may to capture the essence, the voice, the import . . . there aren't enough words to paint love on a page.

Thursday, January 8

Today marks one year since Grandma's lungs turned on her. Today marks one year of birthdays and holidays and conversations I didn't think we'd have. Today marks one year of holding hands and sharing smiles and hearing her say, *"I love you. You're so precious to me."*

I knew today would come. But I thought it would come without Grandma.

Yesterday I gave her fingers an extra squeeze as I slipped them back under her fleecy blanket. This year has been a gift . . . wrapped in layers of grief and joy. I can't begin to tally the minutes and hours I was privileged to spend with Grandma. I can't quantify how much I've needed her.

How can someone be so changed by one year and yet never be more herself?

She's been on hospice and off and back on again.

She's been in the hospital, a rehab place, skilled nursing and her own apartment. She's had full-time caregivers and no caregivers and part-time caregivers. She's diagnosed her own stroke, bounced back from it and never recovered from it. She's lost all sense of time and gained time doctors said she'd never have.

She's been gracious and resilient and patient and funny and stubborn.

Some days I agree with Mom: I'm not sure she knows our names any more. She knows us, but our labels seem to be missing. Then other days I wonder why I would expect to hear my name come off her lips—she's spent decades calling me Cuteheart, Creature or Honey . . . why would I be Kristen now?

Last week I got to spend an hour with her in the morning. After months of her end of the conversation fading to silence, she did most of the talking. Even when the story took a hard turn to fiction she didn't lose her place: she talked about the movie she and Grandpa saw in Ravenna the week before with Uncle Leonard and the old friend from high school she ran into while they were there.

She reflected on how coming from the country and a small high school she knew people would move away, but she didn't imagine she'd ever be as close to any people as she was to those in her class. Yet she moved the farthest and lost touch with all of them and made even closer friends along the way. When Mom arrived at lunchtime Grandma's words had dried up and she listened instead of talking.

The week before, she wrote out my Christmas card. The writing was shaky, but neither did she apologize for it nor did she notice she'd signed it "Great-Grandpap and Mom." Split the difference and the generation is spot on. The twinge I felt was quick. She would find it hilarious that she'd called him Great-Grandpap. He's been Dad and Daddy and Padre and Grandpa and Crap-pa and Great-Grandpa but never any version of Pap. Still the card with her writing meant more than my renewed AAA membership or the check or the books. Another piece of her to treasure, just like the five-year-old voicemail I refuse to delete—I need to hear her and Grandpa singing Happy Birthday to me . . . I need to hold on to the mementos of her.

Friday, January 9

Grandpa called Mom last night. There was more to the routine appointment Grandma had yesterday than he'd indicated on Wednesday. She began coughing earlier in the week. First thing in the morning and right before she goes to bed she coughs. A lot. The doctor listened to her lungs and heard rumblings. Two prescriptions: steroids and heavy-duty antibiotics.

My own breaths shortened. I woke throughout the night with Grandma on my mind.

This morning the sunrise stopped my anxiety in its tracks. Unreal. The colors. The textures. Strange that the most real thing there is— the earth rotating around the sun, the rays of light filtering through the atmosphere—is what seems unreal. The mysterious way viruses and bacteria settle into Grandma's lungs and stump the best western medicine has to offer, that is real every time. But the sun, unreal. I watched the glowing, orange orb peek over the hills. The pressure in my own chest eased.

And then as I drove I smelled a skunk. My pre-coffee, worried-about-Grandma face burst into a smile. Only Grandma and I would welcome skunk odor as a reminder from God that we are His intentional designs and loved beyond comprehension. I breathed deeply and savored the scent. Why is it that it doesn't smell bad to the two of us? Why do we like it? Why do I forget I'm not in control and never have been?

Monday, January 12

"What's new?"

Grandma doesn't know she asked me the same thing moments ago. It was an innocent question then, and it's an innocent question now.

Nothing's new. I smile and joke about my lack of newness as I steer the conversation away from me.

But the question . . . it sits on my tear ducts threatening to cause a spill. Strange—I'm not a crier, yet I'm blinking too fast and swallowing too hard—why? What about *that* question caused tears to spring up?

Deep down, I know what triggers those salty drops. Questions like "what are you doing these days?" force me to confront all the ways I am not where I thought I would be. The present me is not the future me I once envisioned.

There's nothing wrong with the present me. My head knows that. But my pride—oh, my pride!—still keeps score based on the dreams that never materialized. It still whispers the possibilities I mangled into expectations . . . then failed to achieve. I hear the innocent questions and default to how little I have to show for all that's been invested in me.

I don't know how to see the gifts I've been given. The past me didn't and the present me doesn't either. I see the lack and dismiss the bounty. I struggle to value the experiences, the people, the moments against the singleness, the job changes, the loss of dreams.

There's an element of grief coloring the edges of the answer to

"What's new?" But it feels self-indulgent to grieve. The ache is based in perception. Reality looks different. Not bad. Different. Can I mourn what never transpired?

Yet even when Grandma—who has never seen me as a disappointment, who may not know my name but remembers to tell me she loves me—asks the question, I feel the surge of shame. Misplaced, perhaps, but shame nonetheless.

Today I can admit I am living out a different story than the one I anticipated. The plot lines I hoped for may never come to be . . . what does come will be my new, ordinary reality. I can recognize the stirring emotion as that: emotion. Not judgment or truth, just raw response to reality. And that's okay. I'm okay. The nothing-new me will be okay. Maybe I'll even learn to answer without a deflecting joke.

Friday, February 27

Grandma was in rare form today. Jumping in to the conversation, pushing on if Grandpa talked over her, zingers and comebacks, laughing and smiling.

It's hard to say she was her old self again—that self has faded so much—but the spark was strong and steady today. More than an hour after Cameron left Grandma remembered she'd come and was excited about her new job. I doubt she knew Cam used to be her caregiver, but what difference does it make?

A year ago not one of us could have imagined she'd be with us today. I know her quality of life has diminished, but she's still her and she's still here. Even the days when she's quiet and distant and confused it's still her soft hand in mine squeezing back with a strength and a love that belies the angle of descent. How when she's her and she's here can I pray for anything but more of her?

And on the good days the minutes fly by and the years fall away. Her spine remains curled and her shuffle pronounced, but her spirit is unbowed. She is the grandma I adore, the one who makes me laugh and taught me to tease. Her voice is music and her gaze an embrace. Being with her is being loved. Would I be me without these decades of her presence?

Tuesday, March 3

I opened the back hatch of my Scion, and as I did I ran through my list: grab the easel, return it to the events team, head over to my 10:00 a.m. meeting—I froze. On top of my beach chair was a tube of lipstick. And not just any tube, a navy blue tube with a clear lid revealing Wicked-green, Mac Cosmetics Chromacake in Landscape Green lipstick. Grandma's lipstick.

Who else wears Moodmatcher lipstick?

I stared at the tube as though radioactive. Had it been there for the three years I've owned the car? Impossible. It wasn't melted. I picked it up reverently. It must have fallen out of her walker a week and a half ago when I took them home after the birthday party for Uncle Brian and Kevin.

Heading toward my meeting I rolled the tube in my hand. I could picture her at a ladies' luncheon pulling out her green lipstick and applying it as eyebrows arched around the table before furrowing in confusion as the green lipstick went on pink. She's always loved a good gag.

All afternoon the lipstick sat on my desk as a tangible reminder of the joy and humor Grandma finds in life. I've never been sure if she likes the shade or if she wears it for the laugh . . . probably the laugh.

Wednesday, March 4

"My little girl is the bread and butter . . . of . . . she's the bread and butter of . . . Maple Street."

I have no idea what that means, but Grandma got a kick out of declaring me the bread and butter of Maple Street. And if she's laughing, I'm the happiest girl in the world. The other day she said I spoil her—could there be a greater statement?

Last March my prayer was for her not to suffer but also for her to know she was loved and never to feel alone. She doesn't remember those days. She doesn't remember how she tried to find us when we were gone. But I do. I remember her elation at seeing me because she assumed I wouldn't find her.

I saw her every day then, and now it's only three times a week, but now she doesn't worry between visits. She may not know when I was last there, but she knows I'm her girl and I'll do anything for her—I'll spoil her.

My prayers continue to be answered: she knows she's loved, she knows she's not alone, she doesn't remember how much she's suffered. She'll never be who she once was, but she'll always be herself.

This year has been a gift beyond measure. How would life have gone on if we'd lost her last January? What would I have done without her hand to hold and her smile to share and her eye to catch? I can't imagine not having this time with her.

Monday, March 16

Today was a funeral: Wendy's Gramie. It was sweetness and laughter, grief and tears. Loss is always hard—even when we know it's coming. Each hole torn in the heart holds its shape. No one else can ever fill the loved one's place exactly nor do we want them to.

I listened to Wendy and Linda share about Gramie, and I kept thinking about Grandma. What would I say? What would I be feeling? Like them my grieving has already begun but her absence will be no less wrenching when it comes. I held her hand today and teased with her and heard her say she loved me. I listened to her ask me to stay, and still I had to leave. But soon it will be reversed. And what will I do when I can't hold her hand or hear her voice? Will I still be me without her? Will my heart still beat around the void she once filled? It will be such a big, unfillable hole.

Yet she had holes in her heart, and she kept living and loving. She lost parents and eight siblings. She lost two marriages. She lost friends who may as well have been family. And still she embraced life. She didn't need to wear her heart on her sleeve; she was all heart.

Even now when her body and memory fail her, she loves. Oh, how she loves.

Sunday, March 22

It's never going to be easy. Every heart-wrenching phone call that Grandma's taken another turn is horribly hard. Even as I tell myself this is what I wanted—for her to not suffer and to know she's loved—every fiber of my being screams "no—I'm not ready. How will I live without her?"

I rubbed her hunched back as she shuddered against the waves of nausea. Her eyes never opened as I wrapped my hand around hers and tipped the juice glass of Coke, my thumb lifting her chin. They didn't open as I rubbed her arm and teased her about pranks she pulled. They didn't open when she smiled and chuckled at the punch line of our stories.

When it was time to go she tipped her head back for her kiss.

"Goodbye, Grandma. I'll see you tomorrow. I love you so much."

"Oh, I love you so much. You're so special . . . I love you more than you know," she whispered back.

"I love you that much and then some."

Eyes still closed, she smiled.

Twenty minutes later with Brian and Jill she kept her eyes open the whole time and ate Fritos and popcorn. Wonders never cease. But she's so weak. She's slept for two and a half days. Another stroke perhaps? Despite the good oxygen levels and blood pressure, I'm not sure she can bounce back again. It takes all her strength to walk to the bathroom.

As much as I want a painless death—slipping from sleep into Jesus' presence—it feels so close, and I'm not ready. I'm not ready to face life without her.

Monday, March 23

Every time I think I know, I don't. The situation doesn't matter.

I think I've figured out the pattern, the riddle, the reality only to have my solution fail to compute. "The best laid schemes o' Mice an' Men gang aft agley, an' lea'e us nought but grief an' pain, for promis'd joy!"—Robert Burns got it. So did the proverb "The heart of man plans his way, but the Lord establishes his steps."

This is the moment I have. This is the time. This is the reality of my relationships. I can't plan on the presence or the absence of Grandma. The processing and grieving I've already done is important, but it no more prepares me for the reality to come than watching sports makes me an athlete. I haven't figured out grief. I haven't figured out life without Grandma. I haven't figured out dementia or the slow physical decline. I don't know what tomorrow will bring. I don't.

And every time the rug of pseudo-knowledge is pulled from beneath my feet I feel that flash of weightlessness before I crash to the floor. Every time.

So I find myself again wondering how the Grandma of yesterday and the Grandma of today can be the same person. Was today a rally? Is the end bearing down on us? Was the weekend of constant sleep and no strength an aberration to remind us how precious and fleeting the moments are? I don't know. I never will. But I'll always love her; and someday this roller coaster ride of emotions will end, and the next leg of the journey will begin without her voice reminding me, *"I love you. You're so special."*

Thursday, April 2

I've been reading first-person accounts of walking the road of Alzheimer's with loved ones. There are definite similarities and differences to Grandma, though she does not have Alzheimer's. But as I read—and as I journey with Grandma—one thought pesters me: if that's me someday, who will keep my memories? To whom will I give them so I don't lose them? Who will hold my hand or play hymns for me? Who will know I still know their presence even if not their identity?

That might be the hardest part of being single. Should I grow old alone, who will love me?

While Grandma can't track the time, she knows we come—we always come . . . but who comes when there are no children or grandchildren? Who knows how to share the space and be present? Who knows how to morph into long-gone relatives to keep the narrative alive? Who clears the clouds of confusion from the eyes and makes them bright again? Who whispers "I love you, I love you, I love you"? Those unknowns wrench my heart. Maybe they're why my prayer for Grandma has been that she never feels alone and she always knows she's loved. Maybe I'm afraid someday I'll die alone, unsure if I'm loved. Maybe my prayer for her isn't just for her. Maybe I'm praying ahead for the me who can't quite place herself. Maybe.

Saturday, April 11

The extremes: Grandma in her final days, while Aaron, Eli and Kathleen in their first years. Helping Grandma stand and walk—coaching the steps—and helping her in the bathroom and settling her in her chair to try to minimize the pain of her body deteriorating stands in marked contrast to helping Aaron and Eli to walk, changing diapers and soothing pains after falls. With Grandma and Kathleen I helped find their words, listening hard and looking into their eyes to let them know as I repeated back what they meant that whether they are acquiring or losing language they are understandable, their words matter; they matter.

With one I hold the hand because I'm not sure how many more times I'll be able to and because she needs to know she's not alone. With the others I hold hands to steady steps or to offer reassurance they are safe, the dogs are on the other side of the fence. I hold them to let them know in the crush of life they are known and loved. It's the same message for both ends of life: you are not independent. I don't understand what you're feeling and can't articulate, but you are you. You have immense value. You are not alone. I am fully with you.

Monday, April 13 (Kayla's 5th birthday)

The visit with Grandma and Grandpa did not go as planned. Grandma woke up slurring my words back to me, *"Hello, hello."*

She didn't believe me that we'd just arrived; she was sure she'd missed us. Then she wanted to brush her teeth. I couldn't imagine the ordeal of a trip to the bathroom just for clean teeth, so I distracted her while I studied the changed surface of her left eye and the pinprick pupil of her right eye . . . an effect of the morphine? But if we'd taken her to the bathroom to brush her teeth, we would have averted the crisis.

She never mentions her need for a toilet until it's a moment of desperation. Today was no different. Already late before we started. I found her shoes and got them on her though she maintained I put them on the wrong feet. We got her standing and turned her around to sit in her walker. By the time she stood in the bathroom, we were too late. Nature and the medicine to relieve the constipation conspired against us.

There's nothing quite like downplaying an adult's accident while trying to clean her up in a dignified manner. Mom and I did well despite her protestations she was stupid. Mom cut her off the first time. The second time when I said, "Don't say that!" she said, *"I already said it"* like a rebellious child. The hardest part though was she couldn't recall how to clean herself. She got the toilet paper but kept swiping at her thighs unable to follow our coaching.

Somehow, once dressed and in her chair, she put it all out of her mind and was only sad that we had to go.

"I love you, I love you, I love you."

"I love you, I love you, I love you, I love you, I love you, I love—" I interrupted her streak with a kiss.

"Did we get a little boring with our routine?"

Does that mean she remembers this is how we say goodbye?

"Not at all. I love you to the moon and back, Grandma."

Thursday, April 16

The calls, the changes, the new declines—none of them get easier. I was not prepared for the word "unresponsive."

Yet while I was there she was alert, responsive and communicative. Her speech was slurred, but she knew—and I knew—what she was saying. Still noticing and complimenting me. Still joking and making faces.

But some things were different. Her mouth hung open, tongue lolling inside. Her gaze mostly stayed up where the wall and ceiling met. She was watching something we couldn't see. Once she pulled the blanket down and reached out with her left hand. All I caught was *"spooky,"* and she wouldn't repeat it. When Uncle Brian asked her what she was reaching for she said, *"Oh, nothing,"* but it was something.

She drank a little root beer and then a little water. One time she couldn't close her mouth around the straw and sip, but when I took it out and put it back in she knew what to do.

I don't know what any of it means, but it seems the time is coming close. For her to not want to get up or dressed . . . it's not her. The slurred speech, being hot to the touch while still feeling cold—they can't be good signs. And even as I see it, I don't know what to do with it. What does it mean? What do I do? I don't know.

Sunday, April 19

The call came at 6:51 a.m. She was agitated. Grandpa couldn't settle her down. He'd been rubbing her arm and praying with her. Maybe Mom could calm her.

I couldn't tell if she recognized us. She grasped our hands, pressing and squeezing, working her hands up our arms. Sentence fragments and nonsense words swirled amongst the discernable words. Was she talking to us? To them? Whoever they might have been.

She was desperate to relieve her discomfort, but she couldn't. The hospice nurse came and agreed her abdomen was distended. She needed to go, but she could not—because of the kidney stone? Her body went rigid as she grabbed hold of whatever was closest: a hand, an arm, my hair. The woman who could twist an apple apart with her bare hands still had power in her grip. As the urge overtook her, the hand resting on my neck would tighten, thumb and fingers squeezing. Hours later the catheter relieved the pressure and her body began to relax. Nearly twelve hours after the agitation began the anti-anxiety meds arrived, and over the next few hours they began to ease the mental agitation. Sixteen hours after her day began she could rest and even sleep through the night.

Whether it was the mounting fever or the morphine or something else, her lucidity spanned the spectrum throughout the day. As people—Pastor Gary and Joy, the Busses, the Hills, the nurses and caregivers, April, the family—came for minutes or hours she greeted them each then lost them in the swirl.

The hallucinations came in waves. She grasped my arm with both hands, fingers pressing between the bones trying to pull my ulna and radius apart. She picked at her blankets and pajamas and handed me the "trash" to dispose of, not even complaining when I dropped it right on the floor. Over and over she tried to pull off my glasses. Once she tried to detach my ear.

She grabbed my nose, twisting and pulling, fingernails digging in. "Did you need my nose or can I keep it?"

"You only have one?"

"Yep, just the one, so maybe I'll hold onto it."

"Okay."

Several times she reached out and pantomimed bringing a forkful of food to her mouth. At least once she followed up with a full body shudder as though the "food" had nauseated her. Yet if asked, she did not want a bite of anything.

As the Busses—her former boss and his wife—prepared to leave I overheard the following exchange:

"Bye, Maxine."

"Hi!"

"No, I'm leaving."

"That's a funny name."

Late in the afternoon when most of the family was departing,

Grandma looked long into my eyes, *"Why are you here?"*

"Because I love you. I always want to be here with you."

"That's good."

She patted my arm, then gripped it and raised it up as though it was a lap bar on a roller coaster, *"what is this?"*

"Still my arm."

"Oh! *Why do I do that?"* Frustration gave a hard edge to her voice. Her words ran the gamut of her life:

"There were nine of us. I was the youngest."

". . . lab at Magnolia . . ."

". . . flyboy . . . glider . . . flew . . ."

"Pastor Mike . . . Magnolia Baptist Church . . ."

"Brian used to make all his own clothes."

"He's so cute."

"I want to brush my teeth."

". . . taxes . . ."

". . . black coffee . . ."

". . . the car door . . ."

". . . sponge bath . . ."

"I can't even talk."

The farm, her siblings and her parents came up over and over. Conklin made repeat appearances. School—the one-room schoolhouse? high school?—surfaced regularly. Typing, complete with fingers flying through the air, was mentioned more than once.

Lipstick was requested and a hairbrush and mirror. Mom applied the lipstick and brushed her hair. I held the mirror. She was none too pleased with the face she saw.

For a while we were all there: Grandpa, Mom and Dad, Brian and Jill, Jessica and Amy, Kevin and I. Jon was the only missing grandchild praying from four hundred miles away.

As the afternoon wore on Jessica left for work, Kevin headed home and April accompanied Grandpa down to dinner. I held Grandma's hand as those of us who remained prayed together. She stayed quiet as Mom and Dad prayed. While Aunt Jill prayed she whispered to me, *"You're a blessing."* Over and over we thanked God for the gift of our sweet, sweet matriarch and her amazing life. We echoed one another as we asked for her to be welcomed peacefully into His presence and spared pain and agitation in the time she has left with us. In addressing God it was safe to speak words of release. And as we heard one another's hearts, she heard us, too.

Monday, April 20

I feel wrung out. Then smoothed and wrung again. Twisted into a pretzel and squeezed again and again.

I'm not sure why. The past few days have been hard, but this hard? They've been less emotional than many other days in the past fifteen-and-a-half months. And today she was relaxed—thank you morphine and anti-anxiety medication.

There were light moments:

"I can't read the signature."

"The signature?"

"The signature under the moon, low in the sky." She pointed toward the closet.

"Huh, I can't make it out either."

And there were poignant moments. Yesterday she told me she didn't think anyone loved her, but she seemed to believe me as I reassured her how loved she is. Today she told Mom and me she sometimes wonders if God made a mistake putting her where He did. We both stressed how perfectly placed she was and is. Our family wouldn't exist without her.

Something about the waiting, the tension of uncertainty unravels my nerve endings one frayed fiber at a time. I can still be patient and present for Grandma and for Mom—less so for Grandpa—but I feel the tautness, and when I'm alone it collapses. The air rushes out of the balloon. The rubber band snaps and falls limply to the ground.

I had the urge to go into Grandpa and Grandma's bedroom and lie down . . . on the floor. I needed to be on something solid, rigid, formed. It was as though the tendons and ligaments and muscles were on the brink of forgetting how to hold my bones together, and it would all be better if I could lie prone. It was a strange urge. One I didn't heed because as close to caving in as I feel, the need to be with Grandma is stronger. I need to hold her hand, her words, her memory and pour love and peace and comfort into the voids left behind by pain and medications and dying.

Even with dry eyes I feel the hands of grief turning me inside out and wringing and wringing and wringing.

Wednesday, April 22

Yesterday was a good day. I walked in and Grandma was sleeping. Grandpa was at dinner. The caregiver was watching the news. Grandma opened her eyes and smiled at me.

Did I catch her mid-dream? The story she told about apartments and a woman she didn't seem fond of and cars and dirty dishes . . . it was hard for me to follow but clear as day to her. It lasted five minutes. Her longest conversational thread in quite some time.

Sometimes I was Mom:

"Those glasses are so cute on you."

"Thank you."

"Are they new?"

"No."

"When did you get them?"

"Five . . . five and a half years ago."

"Oh! But you don't wear them all the time?"

"All the time I'm awake. I don't wear them to sleep."

"That's wise. They wouldn't be much good then."

I knew I had to be Mom then and in the conversation about whether or not I'd been there earlier in the day. I had not. She insisted I had, and the look of confusion when I said Mom had been there made me realize she thought she was my mom. She couldn't place this "mom" of whom I spoke. I didn't catch it quickly enough to shift from the role of granddaughter to daughter.

But other times she knew just who I was . . . without a name, of course. I haven't heard her say my name in months.

"I remember the day you were born, you little cherub. We were so excited."

That one had to be me. She has no memory of giving birth to Mom, but she was fully coherent for and excited about my birth.

Over and over she told me how full she was. Absolutely stuffed.

She was never quite sure what she'd eaten, maybe one piece of fried chicken, but whatever it was left her uncomfortably full. I smiled and sympathized. No point in telling her it's been more than a week since she's eaten.

"Now let me see . . . what did I do today?"

"Well, this morning you saw the doctor."

"I did." Her brow knitted as she tried to place a doctor's visit.

"Yep, right here, you didn't even have to drive anywhere."

"Oh."

"And this afternoon a nurse was here."

"They buggeth me."

I nearly tipped out of my chair.

"Oh they do?"

She grinned.

A little while later as she searched for words she caught my eye and said, *"I can't get my thoughts together. My mind isn't what it used to be, and it wasn't much—"*

"Don't say that—your mind is still amazing. Maybe it's slowed down a bit, but it's been working hard a long time. It's allowed to be tired."

"It is?"

"It is. I think mine's slowing down and you have a lot of years on me."

"No, no, yours is sharp. And it will be. You're special."

"I don't know—"

"I know."

After a very confusing conversation about Donna—but according to her not any of the Donnas I know—and her twin boys and Grandpa giving them a ride to see their folks, she got a faraway look in her eyes, then turned her full attention to me. She has a way of making sure she has my full attention before she speaks.

"I love you with my whole heart."

"Oh, Grandma, I love *you* with my whole heart. I always have, and I always will."

She smiled. She always responds with how much she loves me, but this was the first time in months that she started the conversation. The best gift she could ever give me. I glanced down at our hands and saw my thumb rubbing the back of her hand in perfect time with her thumb rubbing the back of mine.

We make quite a pair.

Thursday, April 23

I am tired through and through. I'm not sure I've had a thought in a week or two.

I'm tired of trying to puzzle out the meaning of each day and turn. What does it mean that Grandma wasn't eating and now she is? She slept during the day, then she didn't, now she does. I don't know how to make sense of the serpentine twists.

I'm tired of waiting for news. News I know is coming but I don't want.

I'm tired of being present yet feeling unable to plan. It's good to be in the moment, but the uncertainty of the ones to come is exhausting.

I'm tired of going to work and wishing I was somewhere else.

I'm tired of not thinking or observing clearly. I walk, I watch the birds and sky—I see, but nothing connects. I'm not really taking anything in.

I'm tired of being tired. I'm tired of falling into bed utterly spent and waking up desperate for a few more hours of sleep, of stillness. It's not only physical fatigue. It's mental and emotional.

I'm tired of feeling numb. Too many days it's as though I'm watching my own life. I'm here, but I've hit my limit on what I can absorb.

So I bring my tired self. It's all I have. And I sit in stillness—with heavy eyelids—and I hold the exhaustion in open, upturned hands. I've done what I can with it. Now I release it.

Tuesday, April 28

Mom called this afternoon. Grandma was asleep. She slept through Mom's conversation with the caregiver, yet as soon as Mom's lips brushed her forehead with a kiss she awakened. But she was tired. Her eyes closed again, and she slept through Mom's departure.

"And how are you?" I asked.

"I'm okay . . . I got a little teary when I left."

"Mmmm, I can hear it in your voice." A wistfulness and a slight drop in tone slow her words down the smallest fraction of a second when she's fighting off emotion.

"Oh, I'm sorry!"

"No, no, it's okay. I just wanted to make sure you're okay."

One person is dying, but we each experience the process uniquely. What I think and feel—the hole tearing in my heart—isn't the same as what Mom thinks and feels. It isn't the same as what Grandpa or Jon or Kevin or Uncle Brian or Dad or her friends or her nieces and nephews think and feel. The emotion Mom felt as she let go of her mom's hand and slipped silently from the room today is hers alone. We are each walking a solitary journey of slow goodbye. We love the same person—we're losing the same person—but our relationships are remarkably individualized. The lump in my throat may resemble my cousin's, but it is mine alone. She is granddaughter, and I am granddaughter; but we are losing separate relationships that cannot be duplicated with identical roles. Her presence is personal to each of us, and the mark of love she's imprinted on us is without equal.

Grandpa thinks we're getting close. Tonight he told Mom she'd be his first call. Uncle Brian will be the second. And then he uttered words that make it hard to breathe hours later: "I miss her already."

Oh, Grandpa, so do I. So do I.

Friday, May 22

Jessica graduates tonight. Grandma won't be there. She'll sleep through it in her hospital bed in the living room while Grandpa watches the livestream at his desk in the bedroom.

She won't be there . . . but she's here.

We had her for another Mother's Day, and though I saw her and kissed her and held her hand, it didn't feel like Mother's Day. The table seemed empty. A family party—especially one celebrating the moms and grandmas—felt incomplete without Grandma. I know it would have been too much for her. I know we made the right decision to visit her one-on-one or in small groups, but my heart cannot comprehend the changes. Did she eat any of the cookies I made her? Did she look at the poster Dad created and read the messages we wrote on it and know how loved she is? Did she look at the cards taped by her bed and realize how much mothering she has done? I don't know.

We're four days from her ninety-first birthday. A month ago we were sure we'd arrive at the day without her—and we might—but we still have her today. Why am I surprised? Our expectations and assumptions have been wrong over and over again in this sixteen-month odyssey.

I listen to Mom say we've reached a new plateau. I suppose we have. We dip and plateau, dip and plateau, dip and plateau.

On Monday Grandma and I had a long talk—funny how what once would have constituted a brief chat I now label a "long talk"—we revisited her childhood on the farm, and we talked about my childhood. I told her how special I thought I was because I had my own toothbrush at her house, and how patient Grandpa was when we played on the pool table and ruined the bumpers, and how much I loved the permeating aroma of coffee in their home.

On Wednesday I had to manually free my hand from hers each time I got up, she never once willingly let go.

On Thursday talking was too much. She slurred her greeting. She was with me—eyes locked on mine—but she couldn't stay. Three or four minutes and she fell back asleep. I rubbed her hand and chatted with Grandpa. She never heard me leave.

Tonight she won't return to the university where she once worked to watch her granddaughter graduate. But she's here. And while she won't tell Jess how proud she is of her, Jess knows. We all know.

Tuesday, May 26

"Happy Birthday, Grandma!"

"Happy Birthday, Honey."

"Barb Everson sent you a birthday hug and kiss."

"Oh."

Grandma's hands fidgeted beneath the blanket.

"Do you need your hands?" I asked as I pulled the blankets down.

She raised her hands and spread her shaking arms. I blinked in surprise. I said "hug"—she wanted her hug. I leaned over the bed rail and hugged her. She hasn't hugged me in . . . I don't remember my last hug from her.

I swallowed the rock in my throat. Grandma's eyes roved as she clutched my hand.

"How are you?"

"Pretty good, but my mind isn't right."

And that's how our time went. She was alert but agitated. Her conversation darted all over the place. The sentences were complete: subject, verb, object. But I couldn't follow. We sped through time muddying the people and events and blurring lines of logic. I struggled to follow and respond. Her eyes were expectant and then clouded as my faltering responses failed to connect with the words her mind produced. Peppered throughout was her frustration at failing to communicate. She knew she wasn't making sense. She knew the words weren't right. But she still tried.

"I brought you a card. Can I read it to you?"

"Oh, yes."

I held it in front of her, but her eyes never settled on it. As I read the printed words, she murmured. Then I read what I wrote and the blank look remained until the last line: "I love you, I love you, I love you." Her eyes lit up and she smiled at me.

Finally she placed me. And while "birthday" was a concept too hard to grasp, love fit right in.

I stood the card on the end of the server next to the card from Mom and the flowers. Grandma's eyes moved above it to the picture Donna had framed for her birthday.

"Do you see that . . . on the refrigerator?"

"The picture?"

"Yes . . . how's that there?"

"That's the picture of you and Grandpa that Donna had framed for you. I think Grandpa hung it up on the cabinet so you could see it."

She turned her head. I sat back down next to her, then glanced over my shoulder where she seemed to be looking. Nothing.

"Do you see something?"

"Yes, but I misplaced them."

I nodded and blinked the tears back.

When I told her I had to leave to get to a baby shower, her eyes narrowed a bit. The leaving is always a struggle.

"I'll see you tomorrow."

"Okay."

"I love you, I love you, I love you."

She ran her response together. *"I-luh-you-I-luh-you-I-luh-you."*

"Happy Ninety-First Birthday."

"Happy Birthday to you, too."

As my car door closed the tears seeped out. Mom was right. Grandma making it to her birthday wasn't a gift to her. It was a gift to us. A knotted up bow of joy and grief.

Friday, May 29

The cracks in my breaking heart spider into finer and finer lines. Soon it will shatter.

Yesterday Grandma could barely open her eyes and return our greetings before slipping back into a deep sleep. It was a marked change from the sleeplessness and agitation of the preceding thirty-six hours. In some ways I'm grateful the antibiotics for the newest infection and the increased dosage of anti-anxiety meds have freed her from the restlessness and frustration. In some ways.

As we walked to the car Mom broached the subject we've avoided: "I don't know if I should say this . . . I don't know how . . . I'm not sure if we should start thinking about . . . her service."

"I know. I've thought about that, too."

It will be Grandpa's decision. But shouldn't we be prepared?

Mom knows the hymns Grandma would want sung, and the psalm she might want read.

I have the slideshow from their fiftieth anniversary and access to troves of unorganized pictures from the past nine decades. Is it time to start working on a pictorial presentation of her life? Just in case Grandpa wants it shown?

It's strange how Mom has the earliest memories of Grandma. She has known her longer and differently than Grandpa. So as I drove she began making a list of songs she and Grandma used to sing when it was just the two of them. I volunteered Jon or myself to track down recordings and create a playlist of them.

Then Mom asked, "Would you want to share for the grandchildren?"

"I . . . I don't know . . . I don't know if I can make that decision. Should it be Jon? He's the oldest . . . Could I even do it? I think I could, but I'm not sure. I mean, I've thought about it, but I'm not sure."

"It wouldn't have to be just one of you. One of the three of you could share, and Jessie could share for them. Or something," Mom replied.

"I know. And in some ways maybe it makes sense to be me. I mean I think we all secretly think we're her favorite—" Mom laughed before I could finish the word "—not 'favorite' . . . you know—but I think maybe I have known her differently. The three of us knew her as kids in ways Jess and Amy didn't get to, but then maybe lately I've had . . . more time with her."

That's one of Grandma's amazing qualities. I don't think any of us thought we were favored over the others, but we felt we had a special connection with her. And we did—we each did—because she loved us each for who we were as our own unique selves. Not one of us was ever a generic grandchild or held up and evaluated against the other four. She loved Jon with all her heart because he was Jon. She loved Kevin with all her heart because he was Kevin. She loved me with all her heart because I was me. She loved Jess with all her heart because she was Jess. She loved Amy with all her heart because she was Amy. She believed each one of us was special, and she was proud of each one of us. No matter what. Her love was not a finite quantity to be divided but an ever-multiplying source—the more given, the more there was to give.

And that love wasn't restricted to her grandchildren. Everyone who met her believed he or she had a special place in her heart. And each person was right. Her heart had room for everyone.

Tuesday, June 2

"Did I tell you what hospice said yesterday?" Grandpa asked.

I sensed Mom's head shaking behind me as her quiet "no" slipped out. I stayed silent but ready to jump in and distract Grandma if the news was anything less than positive. I hate for her to hear herself discussed clinically.

"Our caseworker—Megan—said they call your mother 'the ultimate fighter.' They've never seen anything like it."

I squeezed Grandma's hand. She smiled at my smile.

She is amazing—and she is making a mockery of the typical hospice rhythms—but I'm not sure if she's a fighter. My first instinct is she's a survivor, but that's not quite right either. She's something different.

She is present. She never quits. She leaves the past in the past and the future in the future. She is now. She's been ready to be with Jesus since long before this "final" season started, but her willingness to go never negated her engagement with the moment at hand. She never stopped living.

Even now, with the dementia and confusion and complete loss of time, she lives. Her ability to track and participate in conversation decreases, but she tries. And maybe that makes it easier—she is present with the person sitting beside her and present on the farm all at the same time. She isn't aware of the catheter or that she hasn't walked in six weeks. She knows she's in bed this second, but where she was an hour ago or will be tomorrow doesn't exist. There is no past or future any more, there is only now.

Is that fighting? Maybe. But it's not aggressive or defiant or angry.

She isn't out to prove anything or defy anyone or claim a victory. She accepts the moment she is in, and she lives it. Nothing more. And absolutely nothing less.

In that sense she is childlike. She trusts—maybe not consciously or intentionally—what needs to be done will be done without concern for the hows and whys and whos. She attends to the present only. She is free to stay in the here and now because she is content to let everything else go. And I'm not so sure that gift can be attributed to the dementia stripping the meaning of time; she knew how to slip the bonds of past and future long before they were ripped away from her.

She isn't fighting or surviving. She has no enemy. She is not afraid of dying. She is not trying to avoid or stall death. She is living.

And that's why hospice can't figure her out. She is a living mystery—emphasis on the living.

Monday, June 8

Yesterday afternoon Uncle Brian, Amy and I loaded six big, plastic totes into the back of my car. A slice of Grandma's history. Aunt Jill added two small boxes: the cards from Grandpa and Grandma's fiftieth anniversary and one labeled "memorabilia."

Armed with a cup of coffee and a vacation day I started small. The memorabilia box. I found pictures from Grandma's childhood on the farm. Pictures of Bernice, too. And mixed amongst Christmas cards, retirement awards and random pictures from the past decade was a blue folder from Grandma's surprise seventieth birthday party in 1994. Out slipped a handwritten note from Jeannien Swift:

Maxine is one of those special persons whom everyone likes and wants to have as their special friend.

She is kind and thoughtful, and wonderful and fun to be with. Always sharing, very caring and excepts more than her part of the responsibility.

She is a real neat gal and I could truthfully go on forever listing her attributes. But—coming back down to earth, after listening to some of

her stories, I find she is human like the rest of us. So—I'm happy to
say that I'm not the only one that does "dumb" things.

Yep, that's Grandma. Captured in less than a hundred words.

And yet as I dig deeper into her history I know her better . . . and
I know her less. Who is this woman?

Today alone I held decades of letters, her ration book from
WWII and a seventh-grade award for spelling. I read words written
by her mom and siblings and in-laws and employers and friends. I
read a neighbor's analysis of Grandma's marriage to Joe and his
opinion of what she needed to consider when deciding to stay or to
go. Not his advice—he was clear—but his opinion on what her
reality and choices would mean for her and for her daughter.

I saw faces long gone—faces to stories I heard in an image-less
void. I caught glimpses of who my sweet grandma was before she
was my grandma: her fun-loving ways, her steely determination, her
selfless generosity, her quiet resolve, her steady pace.

And I wondered at her sacrifice. How did she afford the
correspondence—the time, the stationery, the postage? And the gifts
and pictures? Not to mention the trips to see her family. How did
she do it? And how did she cover for Joe? Were his illnesses and
diets her mother referenced allusions to his alcoholism? If so, did
her mother know? Or did she believe sticking to his diet would heal
whatever ailed him? Did Grandma write the truth to her family? John
Hollingsworth knew. He watched from next door, and he knew
about Joe's continued deterioration in Georgia. He must have
known because he sent that letter she held onto for fifty-five years
and counting. But did her family know?

How much came through in her missives? It's hard to say from
reading the letters she received. She told stories. She sent pictures.
She asked after relatives and recipes. But did she tell how hard her
life was?

For every answered question five more tumble out. For every
insight into her siblings more shadows fall. I lose more and more of
her even as I gain.

Tuesday, June 9

Her heart is getting louder. It sounds different.

I rub her hand through the blanket, and I watch the rise and fall of her chest. Her mouth hangs open, and the skin on her face is drawn and smooth. She looks just like herself, and she doesn't look like herself at all.

At home I look through pictures. Grandma going fishing. Grandma camping. Postwar: some in Michigan, some in California. So young. So full of life. Who took the pictures? Did she ever meet an adventure she wasn't game for?

Even now she is fearless. Not reckless. She is unafraid to live. A child of depression, of war, a woman of independence, of divorce, of single parenting—and not one of the challenges beat her. They changed her, but they never stopped her.

But today the doctor—who makes house calls only for her—heard a change in her heart. Today she could barely wake to greet us. Today she didn't hear us leave.

In the end it might not be the ravaged lungs that stop her. It might be her heart.

Friday, June 12

Grandma is asleep in bed as she's been since I arrived an hour ago. I sit in her pink recliner watching her sleep. At some point I'll get ready for bed and sleep right here across the room from her, but I'm not sure when sleep might come tonight. My mind and heart are racing.

When Mom and I arrived at noon today Grandpa was at the doctor's. Marie seemed quite concerned. He'd fallen three times in the past two days. He had a fever and a sore throat.

A few minutes later he arrived. His voice was squeaky high and the strangest gurgling sound came from somewhere in his throat or chest. He asked me to get him a glass of water to see if he could swallow—earlier it came out his nose, he said with a grin. He took a small sip and appeared to be swallowing before making a bubbling and gagging sound. Water and sputum spurted from his mouth and nose.

Somehow he forced down the giant antibiotic tablet. A great deal of sputum came up, but the pill stayed down.

By three o'clock the trouble swallowing had become trouble breathing. Paramedics transported him to the hospital. Uncle Brian met him there. His fever was 103.2°F. His sputum was brown. The doctor could hear something in his lungs. A machine assisted his breathing. Test after test after test was run. They admitted him.

Mom sat on the edge of the couch. I sat on the edge of the green chair. We leaned in. For seventeen months we'd jokingly wondered what would happen if something happened to Grandpa, but it never seemed possible. And yet . . .

I fumbled for words as I prayed.

Is this what shock feels like? We're simply here. Functioning. Doing what is before us. Moving on autopilot. Making phone calls. Fixing dinner. Sending emails. Waiting for word from Uncle Brian. Waiting. Waiting.

Now I sit beside Grandma. Waiting for news about Grandpa. Waiting for Grandma to need something. Waiting for word. Waiting. Waiting. Waiting.

Saturday, June 13

It's 1:15 a.m. I slept for maybe fifteen minutes between 11:30 and 11:45 before Grandma made noise. It's something between a sigh and a moan. There's a little grimace, and she pulls her right hand up—on her chest, to her collar, near her chin, back down toward her waist—again and again. Sometimes a minute or two of quiet sleep, sometimes fifteen.

When I awakened her to see if she was okay, she said yes. Drink of water? No. Warm enough? Yes. Comfortable? Yes, thank you. But she's not. Is it the kidney stone? Soreness from not moving? Hunger? Dreams? I don't know.

I was beginning to think I could fall asleep about 1:00 when I heard keys at the door. Who comes in now? With keys? If Grandpa got released from the hospital, he'd know the door hasn't been locked in over a year. I reached for the knob as it turned. Georgina, the nurse. Perhaps more surprised to see me than I her.

"I just wanted to check on Mrs. Dagen . . . and Mr. Dagen," she said.

"He was admitted to the hospital. Pneumonia."

"Oh."

"She's been asleep since I got here at seven."

"She's okay," she said. Was that to reassure me or her?

"He'll be in for a few days."

"A little vacation," she said as she showed herself out.

I reshuffled my stack of books. Sleep is a long way off again.

Tuesday, June 16

As each day winds down I find myself composing an email almost equal parts Grandma and Grandpa. The details vary but the message is the same: Grandma is declining, Grandpa is sick; will you pray with me?

Sometimes my requests are clear: good sleep, appropriate medications and responses to it, wisdom for medical staff and for us as family. Sometimes they are simple: pray, please pray. My own prayers—when I can find words at all—tend to be "God, You know. We don't. You love them both more than we do. I'm so glad You're in control, and I'm not."

And it's true. I know less by the day. I may know more medical information than ever, but I don't know what comes next or even what to pray for. Technical knowledge is not wisdom. I cannot control any of this, and I have never been more grateful to not bear that responsibility. The freedom to release the weight of control is priceless. Yet people who don't even know Grandma and Grandpa are praying to the One who is in control. How privileged am I to have people who love me enough to love and pray for those nearest and dearest to me?

Five days after arriving at the hospital Grandpa is still in the Step Down Unit, that ambiguous realm between ICU and standard care.

His voice has returned to its normal range, but his speech is garbled. All the right words come out strung into perfectly appropriate sentences, but he sounds as though his mouth is full of marbles.

Today was better than yesterday. He seemed less confused and agitated though the restraint vest remains in place. His nurse, Anna, took the time to look back and compare his reports and test results for me. The echocardiogram from Saturday and Monday showed the same thing: his heart is in good shape for a man his age, but there is some heart failure and arrhythmia. The elevated enzymes that raised concern about his heart yesterday dropped to almost normal today. Good news. But the pneumonia remains. Sunday's chest x-ray showed more cloudiness. His abdomen heaves with each breath. He is exhausted beyond what sleep can remedy.

And then there's Grandma. Sweet, sweet Grandma. She doesn't know Grandpa's not home. That's been good—she isn't worried, she isn't looking for him, her anti-anxiety meds have been reduced, her routine continues. And it's set her back—it took us two days to discover she missed four doses of antibiotics. Enough time for the infection to surge and ravage her frail body.

Last night the hospice nurse, Lisa, was blunt. She is declining and declining rapidly. Her heart is working too hard with too little success. She's dehydrated and retaining fluids. The doctor today indicated anything could happen at any time. She is declining, but he hesitated from saying more. No doubt her reputation and history of disregarding their prognoses was on his mind.

Three doses back on antibiotics and she was alert and communicative today.

"*I need a pen.*"

"You want a pen?"

"*Yes.*"

I handed her a pen, which she struggled to grip.

"*Paper.*"

"You need paper?"

"*Yes.*"

I grabbed a piece of paper as the pen slipped from her fingers.

"Would you like me to write for you?"

"*Yes.*"

Perched on the edge of the chair I leaned close to catch her quiet, slightly slurred words.

"My friend is a very . . ."

She murmured a few unintelligible syllables.

I read back her dictation: "My friend is a very (pause)?"

"Yes. My friend is a . . . very . . . My friend . . . is a . . . very . . ."

She stared off toward the nurse and caregiver sorting out her medications on the kitchen counter as Mom returned from talking to Aunt Jill in the hall.

Grandma looked at me. I held up the paper and re-read, "My friend is a very."

"Hi, Honey!" she said to Mom, her face erupting in a smile.

"Hi, Mom," Mom smiled back. "Is Kristen writing for you?"

"Yes."

And that was it. I don't know what her friend was, but it was important for it to be noted, and it was noted.

Last night's wondering about our possibility of a double funeral seemed less likely today, but still I wonder. My grandparents—two of the pillars of my life—are forever changed. And the day is barreling toward me when I will be facing life without them.

Friday, June 19

"I wonder what the Lord has in store for us today?"

"I don't know. I think they've been good things so far."

"Probably."

Last night was the first night none of us was with Grandma. Lynn stayed. And Marie will be there the next two nights. The caregivers seem skeptical of our abilities despite five good nights and one night of some agitation for Grandma. But the break for us—having them there—is good. We are all weary and running ruts between hospital and hospice.

Grandma was good this afternoon. Alert, understandable, comfortable.

Mom and I left her and headed to the hospital. An all too familiar new routine. The labyrinthine halls no longer a confusing maze.

Grandpa was asleep but heard me greet the cleaning lady as I passed her. He blinked his heavy eyelids.

"Hi Grandpa."

His eyes—watery and red—found us. No smile. He was uninterested in opening the package I brought. None of us had thought to pick up their mail for a week. I emptied their overstuffed box this afternoon and delivered what appeared important. He motioned it toward the stack of papers and books he'd requested but never touched.

He gave us the report. He is exhausted and the cardiologist doesn't know why. He ate cottage cheese and fruit for lunch. He took three steps during physical therapy, couldn't do any more and got back in bed. He's so tired. He was a little easier to understand today. His speech was slightly less garbled, a few less marbles in his mouth.

The nurse came in and filled in some details. Physically he is improving. Yesterday's progress on the pneumonia front continues today. After the bad night on Tuesday night when he had to be repeatedly suctioned and put on high-flow oxygen, they were able to return him today to the low-flow oxygen. But she cautioned the actual oxygen levels couldn't be lowered despite the less obtrusive delivery system. He did take a few steps. He did have a nutrition drink for breakfast and ate a little at lunch. The exhaustion is the biggest concern. The nurses are trying to get the doctors' okay to take him out in a courtyard to get a change of scenery, some sunshine, stimulation and maybe motivation to stay awake.

After she left Grandpa laid out his plan. "Joanne . . . I've got a long road ahead of me."

"I know Daddy. Brian and I have already talked about that. We're hoping you'll be able to go back to Town and Country for rehab in skilled nursing."

"Well, yes . . . I'm going to Town and Country. But I've been thinking . . . they could put me in skilled nursing and Mother . . . I want us to be side-by-side. We started this together . . ." Eyes closed. Deep breaths. "It's funny. She might live longer than me."

"That's not the kind of funny we like," I countered.

Mom added, "Not funny. Ironic."

"Ironic. It's ironic," he agreed.

"Well, right now we just need you to keep getting better," she said as she squeezed his hand.

"I'm trying. I'm doing everything I can."

"I know. You're a fighter—"

"I'm fighting," he murmured.

"—you and Mom. You two could take on the world."

"Take on the world? I don't know about that."

"Oh, the world is afraid of you two, Grandpa."

His eyes were still closed as we left. He raised his arm in a weak wave. What does it mean for him to be physically improving but increasingly fatigued?

Thursday, June 25

As I make the walk between independent living and skilled nursing I catch the eye of every resident I pass and offer a smile and a quiet greeting. It's important in ways I can't explain. As my own grandparents' dignity hangs in the balance, I can affirm the dignity of others. I can see and convey value to the ones I don't know even as I struggle to meaningfully pour honor into my grandparents.

Everything is backwards. The one on hospice is in the apartment in the independent side. The "healthy" one is undergoing three types of therapy a day in skilled nursing.

I sit at bedsides and hold hands and weave stories about deer stripping the peach tree in my brother's backyard while my eyes measure the rate and effort of each breath. I gauge the coloring and clamminess of the skin, the focus and dilation of the pupils, the strength in the hand in mine as I fight to divert attention from physical deterioration to something more cheerful. I do it for each of them because they both need to know their proximity to death has not changed their proximity to love.

I smile and I tease because this is what we do; this is who we are. We are family. In health and in sickness we show up, we crack jokes, we tell stories. We celebrate. There are no cakes or streamers or witty greeting cards today, but still we celebrate. We claim victory for the tiniest things: a sip of water, a shaky step, a hint of appetite.

And as I move through the hallways from one grandparent to the other each step echoes a reminder: I am blessed to have them. So I raise my eyes to meet each set of eyes I pass and let the smile on my lips curl the grief in my heart to joy.

Time is not counting down to death. Time is counting up from birth.

Sunday, June 28

"Grandma, do you know how much I love you?"

"Uh, twenty . . . twenty . . . nine . . . the wind blows."

"Sounds good."

"Was I wrong?"

"I was going to say all the grains of sand on the beach."

"Really?"

"Really."

Tuesday, July 7

Grandpa entered skilled nursing seventeen days ago, and he's finagled almost a half dozen visits to Grandma in that time. How the rules get bent for the two of them I do not know. Supposedly only family members of record can sign him out and take him to see her, yet April came to visit and took him on Sunday. I suppose all the mornings washing and curling Grandma's hair and applying her makeup earned the label of family for April. Her timeline with them is shorter, but her love for them is just as real.

And maybe it's that. Maybe I'm awed not so much by how loved they are but by whom they are so loved. Former caregivers. Staff and employees at the retirement home. Nurses. My childhood friends. People who haven't seen them in years and people who met them mere months ago adore them.

Grandpa fights to get better, to return home. Grandma keeps living. And people come like clockwork to visit. Jon and Angela drive down to see them and announce great-grandchild number four will be here in six months. The Hills drop in. Terry hears Grandpa's voice from the hall and pops his head in to get the latest news. Chaplain John makes the rounds. Chef Jeff comes by. Cards arrive from near and far.

Even as I'm less convinced Grandma knows who I am, she is as endearing as ever. Yesterday she smiled and tried to respond appropriately, but my face and words didn't seem to click with her. But when I said "I love you, I love you, I love you" she chuckled in recognition.

"Did you just laugh at me?"

"Would I laugh at you?"

"Yes, yes you would!"

She grinned the widest grin I've seen in a long, long time. She does know me.

Thursday, July 9

Sometimes I get the answers I want. And I don't know what to do with them. I don't know how to reconcile the answers with the collateral.

I'm relieved to hear Grandpa and Grandma will be together again. I'm even relieved to hear it will be in skilled nursing.

But . . . Grandpa thinks he's getting released from skilled to return to their apartment in independent living. He's not. He isn't progressing well enough. He might never live in the apartment again.

But . . . Grandma reentering skilled nursing means she will never leave it alive. She is stable. Her systems are working and keeping her alive. The doctors are baffled by her, but she is dying. She will never get out of bed. She will never feed herself again. She will never dress herself. She will never be well. She will die in skilled nursing—that day may come in a bed beside Grandpa, or it may come after he has left for assisted living . . . he has that possibility; she does not.

Grandpa believes he has a meeting to hear good news today. I'm afraid he is going to feel ambushed when he wheels in expecting good news and hears the opposite . . . and finds out his children already knew. That's killing me. How do I reconcile knowing before he does what decisions are being made without his knowledge? How do I honor his dignity while more and more of his life is out of his hands? How do I support him as his world is flipped again?

And then there are the details. What happens to their apartment if neither of them can ever return to it? What do we do with their things? What is the likelihood of Grandpa moving to assisted living? What is the timeline? What are the ramifications? What are the financial, emotional and relational costs?

We haven't been able to answer these questions for the last nineteen months. I don't know why I think now will be any different.

I wanted them to be together. I wanted them to have more care. I wanted him to be in assisted living where people will keep track of medications and appointments and make sure he's using his walker. I wanted any trace of caregiving to be removed from his shoulders. I wanted all that. But I didn't want him to be hurt. I didn't want his hope to be crushed. I didn't want him to feel betrayed. I didn't want her to be left behind.

Now I don't see how I can have both. In getting what I wanted—in Grandma moving to skilled nursing, and in him being unable to return to the apartment—he is losing. He's losing independence. He's being discussed instead of being in the discussion. He's losing his choice and his voice.

The things he did to Grandma are being done to him. And it is agonizing to see it coming and be unable to protect him. I've failed them both. Her from him, him from us, both of them from the system.

Monday, July 13

Friday was hard.

Grandma's hospice-provided hospital bed was too wide to fit through the door, so she couldn't be wheeled from the apartment to skilled nursing in it. She was moved into a Geri chair instead and brought to her new room. There was a delay in getting her variable pressure mattress pad transferred, which meant more waiting in the chair in a position she wasn't used to being in.

Her discomfort—and my inability to help her—set everything in me on edge. Did no one care that she didn't understand what was happening? Where was the urgency to get her transitioned? The swirl of people and technical jargon and unfamiliar surroundings and faces did nothing to settle her . . . or me.

I fear they look at her and see a body and a checklist of tasks to fulfill their duties. I see a soul deserving the utmost care and compassion.

The CNA connected her air mattress and brought in the Hoyer lift. They fitted the sling in place and raised Grandma from the chair, her frail body suspended in midair. Even a few years ago such a ride would have elicited a smile and a joke from her, but now it is too much. Once lowered to the bed her eyes showed fear and confusion.

I left the room filled with apprehension. After months of caregivers watching each breath and spooning water into her dry mouth, would she be forgotten in her quiet corner? Who would coax her to eat? Had this all been a mistake?

But Saturday came, and the news was good. Grandma ate a big breakfast. Her steady routine of oatmeal for breakfast and noodles for lunch with nutrition drink supplements has broken. She's back to pureed food, but she's also back to three meals a day and variety. She's eating well. And while she may not have the will to ask any more, she's getting her teeth brushed again. A detail so small yet freighted with dignity.

She smiled at me and wanted her kiss. She recognized our parting and was quick to respond:

"I love you, I love you, I love you."

"I love you . . . I love you . . . I love you."

Yet they gave her anti-anxiety medication Saturday night and she was still asleep at noon on Sunday. Grandpa said she ate her breakfast—pureed French toast with syrup—without ever opening her eyes. He doesn't seem to understand that if she pulls her legs up and is a bit unsettled it doesn't inherently mean she's agitated and needs to be medicated. He doesn't seem to realize how powerfully medications affect her weakened body.

But they are together. And he sat beside her and listened to her nonsensical reminiscing about her brother John and living in

Westchester. He rubbed her arm and talked to her. He watched her sleep and opened the window so they could have fresh air.

If I squint, I can see it's as it should be. They are together. They are safe. They are loved. And isn't that what I've prayed for all along?

Friday, July 24

Knowing what's coming does not soften the blow. I cannot pray for her to die. I cannot. But I cannot pray for her to live. I can only pray for her to be safe in Jesus' arms wherever He chooses to embrace her.

Lisa—the hospice nurse—was so calm and gracious today. Somehow hearing her say that Grandma's organs are beginning to fail was almost a comfort. She's been in so much pain the last week. And today she wasn't moaning. She wasn't hurting. But the sound of her battling to breathe put my own lungs in a vise. Watching that sweet, sweet chest heave far too rapidly almost undid me. Even Grandpa seemed a little teary.

She hears us. She murmured when Jess and I told her how much we love her. She tried to open her eyes when we kissed her goodbye.

But there's nothing I can do for her. I would do anything. And there's nothing.

Sunday, July 26

She was so peaceful today. Comas will do that, I suppose.

The timeline is getting fuzzy in my head. Is today the third day without food or fluid or has it been three days? Did she have anything Friday morning? Or was whatever she choked on Thursday night her final sustenance?

A nurse told Uncle Brian we're looking at two to three days. Is that a maximum, a minimum? Does it matter? She isn't eating. She isn't drinking. She isn't in pain. Her body is slowing in one final concerted effort. Even as I watch her rapid breathing I know it means her heart is working less effectively, she's receiving less oxygen for each of those inhalations.

I wrap my hand around hers and balance on one foot to lean over the rail and kiss her too warm forehead. I whisper, "Goodbye, Grandma. I love you."

I meant to say it in triplicate so she would know it was me . . . but it only came out once before tears threatened to spill over.

Monday, July 27—1:37 a.m.

Grandma met Jesus face-to-face. She will never suffer again. A few minutes before midnight July 26, 2015. Ninety-one years and two months on earth, and now eternity stretches before her.

Grandpa called Mom, then Uncle Brian. I texted the boys. Mom and Uncie talked.

Mom and Dad and I sat in the dark for an hour and forty-five minutes. Who needs to be called? What will our days look like now? When will the service be? Where?

I didn't realize she was being cremated. I guess we don't need to pick out clothes. Cremation has always bothered me, but it doesn't seem to matter now. That body isn't her. Not at all.

Her appearance changed so much these past few months. It's not how any of us want to remember her. But I do want to remember leaning over her bed and kissing her warm forehead and whispering goodbye less than twelve hours before she slipped the shackles of her failing—failed—body and met her Jesus.

I saw her so often the changes weren't so hard to reconcile with the image that will remain in my mind. I don't think it will be the end-of-her-life body I picture. I hope the image will match the memories and stories. And the memories and stories will not be from the five hundred sixty-five days—the one year, six months and nineteen days—of our long goodbye. There were many good memories in those days, but the stories I will relive most often will be from earlier years.

Somehow life will go on. Decisions will be made. And in the next days and weeks my every plan will not be contingent on Grandma. That doesn't feel real yet. Maybe none of this feels yet. How could it? How can it be that my sweet, sweet Grandma is gone? How can it be that I won't rush from work to hold her hand and whisper "I love you, I love you, I love you"?

Monday, July 27—later in the day

Uncle Brian called the funeral home. We need five things: durable power of attorney, her social security number, her parents' birthplaces, a recent picture and clothes. I pulled out my laptop and looked up her parents' birthplaces. John Borgman was born in Michigan, no city given. Emma Carpenter was born in Marion, Wisconsin.

We headed to the apartment. Uncle Brian found the power of attorney documentation in a box on the top shelf of the closet while Mom and I selected clothes: a jacket, black slacks and a white turtleneck because Grandma was always self-conscious about her neck. The jacket is elegant and bright—three-quarter sleeves, black and white floral with splashes of blue and purple—it's beautiful, like Grandma. We tucked a pair of silver earrings in the jacket pocket. The graveside and burial will be before the memorial service. I'm not sure why we're worrying about her clothes . . . I guess this is what we do.

We returned to skilled nursing.

The bedspread scratched the backs of my bare legs. The air stilled. The temperature inched up degree by degree.

I listened to Grandpa. I'd know that voice anywhere. The words slipped past me but the cadence soothed. Then Mom's voice picked up next to me. I heard her—I did—but I missed her words, too.

And then it was my turn. I thought I could. I started. Did I get out a whole word or was it only a syllable before my throat constricted and my voice cracked? By the second word a tear splashed off my arm. Uncle Brian's chair scraped across the floor and I felt his hand on my knee. Mom's arm wrapped around my shoulders and my head nestled into her neck.

I'd been fine all morning. I hadn't cried when we discussed cremation versus burial or why Grandma couldn't bear the thought of cremation after she'd watched her sister burn to death. I hadn't cried when we discussed the services or Grandma's favorite hymns. I hadn't cried when Grandpa recounted the nurse discovering Grandma had stopped breathing or described the man from the funeral home arriving at 1:30 in the morning to take her body. I'd participated in the conversation for hours without a tear.

But as soon as I began to pray, the tears came.

I cried for the same reason I could hold it together as a child—after an injury or insult—until I heard the sound of my mom's voice. My determined resolve and stubborn stoicism melted in the safety of her presence.

And in the presence of my God—even without the sound of His voice—I crumble in the security of His love. The façade of self-reliance is stripped away and my commingled joy and grief is laid bare.

It's the best, most frustratingly ill-timed reflex: safety, love, tears.

I choked out the words, letting them pool in Jesus' hands. I don't know what I said. I may have stopped mid-sentence. I squeezed Uncle Brian's hand to let him know my words had dried up.

A breeze wafted through the open window. I heard him say, "Amen." I grabbed a tissue, took a deep breath and turned back to my family . . . the one in which it's safe to be real.

Saturday, August 1

I'm drinking my coffee extra-creamy today. Somehow I think it would make Grandma smile. She drank black coffee because Aunt Sally stopped buying cream—isn't that a perfect reason for me to indulge in extra cream?

I sit in the living room bathed in natural light to avoid the thousands of pictures strewn across the family room floor and the sunroom table. I love the pictures. I asked for them. But they overwhelm me.

Plumbing the depths of Grandma's life in pictures is a rich expedition, but at this moment I can't face the piles: pictures to send to relatives and friends, pictures to divide amongst my brothers, parents, uncle and cousins, pictures piling up for Grandpa's slideshow . . . I hear the brief falter in my voice when I explain that pile to Mom. There's nothing wrong with it, but what does it say that I'm preparing for another service—another memorial—for a man very much alive?

My body feels much too big and much too small to contain me. I feel bound and constrained. I feel unhinged and expansive. Cataloging a life, a person's memories and presence—condensing ninety-one years into a few moments of images flashing across a screen—is a heavier task than I could have imagined.

Last night Mom sat on the floor with me, our hands full of pictures. Split-second decisions: picture of Kevin, Nancy and Brian—mail to Nancy? give to Brian? give to Kevin? A flick of the wrist and it's in a pile. Then as she continued sorting pictures into piles I began shuffling the Grandma pile into chronological order and filing each image in with the hundreds of other potential slideshow pictures.

I'm not sure how long Mom stared at the picture before she found her voice and passed it to me. Grandma's wedding picture: a close-up of her with her first husband. We tracked down his name on Wednesday—Duane "Buzz" Cardy—on a sheet torn from a legal pad and tucked into my Michigan album from 1998. And now in perfect writing on the back of the picture we have a date: May 10, 1947. Sixteen days before her twenty-third birthday.

It won't go in the slideshow, but I slid it into the 1940s section. So far it's the only 1947. I fit it between 1946 and 1948.

Less than an hour before, Mom had called Grandma's cousin, Bob, to tell him about Grandma. He's the last one living from that generation. The man who introduced his cousin Maxine and his WWII service buddy Buzz. Time crashes down on me sixty-nine years later.

Friday, August 7

Yesterday was the day.

Family—and a few select friends—gathered at the graveside. In the humid mid-morning, under scattered clouds, Uncle Brian spoke.

Grandpa, Mom, Jerry Hill and Uncle Brian prayed. And while great-grandchildren played a blue casket was lowered deep into the ground.

Hours later the small church was filled beyond capacity: two hundred thirty people to celebrate Grandma. It was a family affair. Grandpa welcomed everyone. Aunt Jill, Jess and Amy sang. Kevin read Psalm 23. Jon prayed. Dad led us in singing "The Old Rugged Cross." Mom gave the eulogy. I shared. Uncle Brian brought the message.

Mom captured her mom so well:

> Again, thank you so much for being here. She loved you all so much and it is our delight to have you here. And I hope you'll indulge me for just a few minutes while I share about her amazing life.
>
> A family was made complete on May 26, 1924, when Maxine Ardith Borgman was born, the youngest of John and Emma Borgman's nine children. They lived on a farm in rural Michigan, on the outskirts of a very small town named Conklin.
>
> Although life was hard in a farm family, with lots of chores and no amenities, Mom had nothing but fond memories of farm life. She adored her older siblings. They, in turn, doted on her when they were at home. Many of them were living in town by the time she was old enough to remember.
>
> She attended a one-room school, which was on the corner of her parents' property. One of her chores was to be the first one at school each morning to get the coal furnace going and the room heated before her beloved teacher, Mr. Kelly, and the other children arrived. She loved school; she loved learning.
>
> After eight years at her homey, little school, she went on to Ravenna High School, in the neighboring town, where she made lots of new friends. She loved being part of the Glee Club, and to her mother's great dismay my mother chose to

take shop class with the boys, rather than joining her girlfriends in home economics. In spite of this, she went on—as most of you know—to become a fabulous cook, baker and homemaker in later years. However, she never learned to sew!

She graduated from Ravenna High in 1942 and was thrilled to go to Business College at the behest of her eldest brother, Byron, also a lover of learning. But prior to starting Business College, she was given a trip to California in the summer of 1942 to visit her older sister, Sally, who worked in Los Angeles. This was her first taste of Southern California—well probably of anywhere other than Conklin—and she loved it!

After Business College, she worked at Continental Aviation as a secretary while living with her eldest sister and her family in Muskegon, MI. Although sister Sally eventually returned to Michigan, Mom was drawn back to California where she moved after the war years.

She was hired as a secretary at General Foods in Los Angeles, made many life-long friends and met her husband. They were married on July 28, 1951.

One year later, on August 16, 1952, she gave birth to me. We resided in Westchester in a wonderful neighborhood where the coffee pot was always on and usually a neighbor lady or two were in our kitchen for a morning visit.

By August of 1958, our little family was on the move, transferred by General Foods to Dunwoody, Georgia. Mom, with her engaging personality, soon had many new friends and carried on the coffee klatch tradition in her new neighborhood. And although I loved it and it seemed like an idyllic life to me, Mom's marriage was ending, and we were on our way back to California.

Mom handled single-parenting so beautifully that I actually thought I was the luckiest girl among all my girlfriends because I had my wonderful mother all to myself. She carved out a sweet life for us in Gardena. She worked as an executive secretary at Mechanical Specialties and supported us with the help of amazing friends since we had no family within 2,500 miles.

Mom's life changed dramatically and wonderfully when she met Art Dagen at a Christmas party that our landlords held for their tenants. He lived in our same small, little apartment building. And when she met him she wanted to introduce him to her niece, but he had eyes only for her!

They were married on April 7, 1962. In 1963 my brother, Brian, was born and our family was complete Now, having outgrown our apartment, we moved to Anaheim with the waves of families settling in Orange County at that time.

For the next 46 years Mom enjoyed making their house a welcoming home, treating her neighbors like family, serving the Lord at Magnolia Baptist Church as a secretary and in many lay ministries and also served for several years at Biola University. She was a friend to everyone she met. Her guest room was always open. One morning Dad even found a young woman sleeping in their guestroom. When he told mom, she went to check to see who it might be and then remembered that she had offered the room to a friend from Biola, who apparently had let herself in with the hidden key the previous night when my mom and dad were out for the evening. Everyone knew about the hidden key, so it wasn't really hidden!

No one enjoyed a joke or prank more than Mom. Some of you may have been the recipients of a plant—Darrell— potted in an old toilet and left on your front porch or her famous food tricks: mashed potatoes served with chocolate syrup as dessert for the unsuspecting, rubber candy mixed in with the good stuff for guests, the ever-popular cotton ball cookies on April Fool's Day. She knew how to have fun!

When Ed and I married and a few years later Brian and Jill married, she embraced her new role as mother-in-love. She hosted more holiday meals, birthday parties and family dinners than you can imagine.

One of her greatest joys was becoming a grandmother, first to Jonathan in 1976 and then Kevin in 1979 and Kristen in 1980. And just when my children were in their early teen years, along came Brian's Jessica in 1992 and Amelia in 1995, much to Mom's delight. She never missed a milestone of those grandchildren's lives, attending Little League games and band concerts and graduations.

Even when Brian and his family moved to the Czech Republic in 1997 to serve as SEND missionaries, Mom and Dad traveled there to make memories with them.

When her great-grandchildren arrived she was over the moon—first Kayla in 2010, followed by Norah in 2012 and her first great-grandson, Aaron, in 2014. It was such a joy to watch Mom watch them! Her eyes were always on the children.

Leaving her home to move to Town and Country Manor in 2009 was very hard for her, but she did so graciously and without complaint, as was her nature. Once again, Mom made friends and eased into this new phase of life.

In January of 2014, when Mom developed double pneumonia, we began the difficult process of saying goodbye to her. She battled valiantly for life, over-coming setbacks that earned her the title of "The Ultimate Fighter" from her hospice nurses, continuing to always put others first, surprising us with her witty comebacks, and that smile. Who can forget that smile?

Just before midnight, on Sunday, July 26, Mom took Jesus' hand, as He welcomed her into His paradise. We miss her more than we can say, but we are so thankful for her 91 years of love and devotion to her family and her friends and her Savior.

She treasured her relationships with each of you. Thank you for loving her and for honoring her with your presence today.

And after the slideshow played, it was my turn:

My name is Kristen, and I am one of the five most privileged people on the planet. My two older brothers—Jonathan and Kevin—and two younger cousins—Jessica and Amelia—and I are Max's grandchildren.

I didn't realize Grandma wasn't like all the other grandmas.

Didn't every grandma keep a pair of fake, bloodshot eyes on hand to pop in before opening the door?

Didn't every grandma hide her rubber chicken in random places around the house? Oh, not every grandma *had* a rubber chicken?

I thought they did. Mine did.

As a child I begged her to teach me how to make her face that you saw. She taught me how to use my finger to dry my teeth and roll my upper lip under, how to pinch and keep my nose closed, and how to cross my eyes. That was the face she and another secretary perfected in the church office where they worked. Wouldn't every pastor appreciate being greeted by those faces?

I practiced and practiced the face. My brother—Kevin—had her timing and ability to pull a prank, but I had her face.

Everyone loved Grandma. She made friends on planes and in grocery store lines. She never met a stranger.

And though I was used to non-relatives calling her "Aunt Max" or being part of holidays and family occasions, it caught me off guard when one of my friends started calling her "Grandma."

I was fine sharing her . . . in the form of hugs at church. But to share her title was a little unsettling. Especially because my friend's own grandmothers were active presences in her life. Why did she need a third?

But, even in my selfishness, I knew it meant something amazing. I knew it meant this woman who loved me was so generous in her love that she had enough to reach beyond our family and pull in others. Not because they were lacking in family, but because there's always room for more family to speak words of truth and encouragement.

And as junior high students was there anything my friend and I needed more than a grandma or three in our corner?

I spent the five hundred sixty-five days from the time Grandma went into the hospital with double pneumonia on January 8, 2014, until the day she stepped into eternity on July 26, 2015, thinking and writing about Grandma and reflecting on what it was that made her so special.

And one quality kept coming to mind. It's the presence phenomenon. Grandma had a way of being fully present. She was fully in the moment, in the conversation, in the room—whoever was with her, as you know, felt he or she was the only person in the world. Grandma was a good conversationalist, but she was a great listener. I don't think she was ever so eager to make her next comment that she stopped listening to the person talking to her. She didn't monopolize conversations or play conversational one-upmanship. She listened with empathy and celebrated or mourned as appropriate.

So today we memorialize one person, but we each experience her loss uniquely. What I think and feel isn't the same as what Mom thinks and feels. It isn't the same as what Grandpa or Jon or Kevin or Dad or Jess or Amy or Uncle Brian or Aunt Jill or Wendy or Angela or all of you her friends, her nieces, her nephews think and feel. We are each walking a solitary journey of goodbye. We loved the same person—we lost the same person—but our relationships were remarkably individualized. The lump in my throat may resemble my cousin's, but it's mine alone. She is granddaughter, and I am granddaughter, but we lost separate relationships that cannot be duplicated by identical roles, and that's a gift. Grandma's presence was personal to each one of us, and the mark of love she's imprinted on each of us in this room is without equal.

That was one of Grandma's amazing qualities. I don't think any of us thought we were favored over the others (or maybe we did), but we each felt we had a special connection with her. And we did—we each did—because she loved us each for who we were as our own unique selves. Not one of us was ever a generic grandchild or held up and evaluated against the other four. She loved Jon with all her heart because he was Jon. She loved Kevin with all her heart because he was Kevin. She loved me with all her heart because I was me. She loved Jess with all her heart because she was Jess. She loved Amy with all her heart because she was Amy. She believed each one of us was special, and she was proud of each one of us. No matter what. Her love was not a finite quantity to be divided but an ever-multiplying source—the more given, the more there was to give.

And that love was not restricted to her grandchildren. Everyone who met her believed he or she had a special place in her heart. And each person was right. Her heart had room for everyone.

Thank you for being here with us today.

When the service ended we fell into the arms and smiles of so many people we hadn't seen in years—maybe decades—and those who walked so close to us through the eighteen and a half months of goodbye. The Holtmanns flew in from Chicago, just for Grandma's service. Three out of four Wittman children with their own families were present. Mom's childhood friend, LaVonne—

who invited her to church and began Grandma and Grandpa's journey with Jesus—was there. Three of her caregivers came. So, so many people folded into the fabric of our family over the decades because of Grandma's magnetism were drawn back to mourn her loss and celebrate her life.

It was a party all about people—about relationship. It was a party she would have loved.

Saturday, August 8

Grandpa is home. June 12 he went into the hospital. June 21 he went to skilled nursing. July 10 he and Grandma were moved into the same room together in skilled nursing. July 26 Grandma went home to heaven. August 7 Grandpa went home to their apartment.

Stepping through the door and seeing him sitting at his computer seemed strange for a moment. But then it seemed right. Life goes on.

And I'm glad. I'm glad Grandpa and Grandma were together at the end. I'm glad Grandma didn't die in the hospital. I'm glad Grandma didn't die at home.

Everywhere and everything reminds me of her. But walking into their apartment—without the hospital bed and oxygen machine and smell of looming death—feels right. I'm reminded of her in good ways and not in last days' ways. I can revel in the associations that flood me with memories of my sweet grandma. I can remember that even in her physical absence I am her granddaughter, always and forever.

Monday, August 17

I opened the envelope and pulled out the card: a sympathy card. The kind I hate buying and writing because they always seem inadequate and . . . sad.

But this one was perfect. I don't remember what it said—those minutes and days and weeks escaped without leaving detailed memories behind. But the card was perfect because someone bought it and wrote a message in it and addressed it and mailed it. To me. And even if I couldn't process the words, I could hold that card and know it was real. My loss was real. Their compassion was real.

And it was perfect because it's the only one I received.

I received numerous texts and emails and Facebook messages and voicemail, but I can't stop thinking about that solitary card. As meaningful as the other communication was—and it was—it mostly disappeared into the digital haze. I can't pick it up and hold it and absorb the known-ness of the handwriting and be awash in the memories and the tangible friendship the overpriced paper and ink evokes.

Someday after a new normal becomes real I will stand in a store and select a card. And as I hold it I will remember being saturated with grief, fingering a card and feeling the weight of friendship; and that memory of love will propel me to seal my own love in an envelope and mail it away as an act of presence for someone else buffeted by the tempest of loss.

Wednesday, August 19 . . .
my first birthday without Grandma

Grandpa called while I was in a meeting. He left a voicemail, but I got busy dealing with the fallout of announcing my resignation and didn't listen to the message. Mid-afternoon I remembered his call.

Sometimes when I check my voicemail it prompts me to review saved messages. I don't know how it decides when to replay them. I don't know how to access them unless it does it for me. I never listen to them, but I like that they're there.

Today the old messages started playing unprompted. The first one began—my brother seeing if I was free for lunch eight years ago—and I punched in the code to skip and resave it.

Then the second one started and I froze. I knew what it was. I have the order of the messages memorized, but I had no idea how shocking it would be to hear Grandma singing "Happy Birthday" to me . . . on my birthday. Rooted in place I listened to my grandparents' duet. And then—for the first time in six years—I listened to the rest of the message.

"That oughta make your day, Honey, (chuckle) or ruin your day, Honey." Her voice lilted up. I could hear her smile.

Grandpa chimed in, "We hope you have a wonderful day, and, uh, Kristen, I have a box of books out on the back patio here, and if it's all right with you, I'm going to inventory 'em and send you a list of 'em that you can decide which ones of 'em you want me to keep and the rest of 'em I'll get rid of. So, uh, I might get started on that today, so that's just a thought. But we hope you have a wonderful, wonderful birthday, and I don't know what you're doing but enjoy."

"We love you very much—"

"That's for sure."

"—Thanks for being our granddaughter, okay? Bye-bye."

"Talk to you later. Bye-bye, Honey."

I'm not sure how long I stood at the corner outside the restroom. Did the next two saved messages play? I don't know. I started listening again when Grandpa's voice jolted me back to today.

"Hi, Kristen, this is Grandpa. I'm just calling to wish you happy birthday. I would sing, but without Grandma it wouldn't be too good, so all I can do is say happy birthday, I love you, you're a special girl and look forward to seeing you again. Okay? Have a wonderful day—as I know you will—you'll be well treated today, I'm sure, and, uh, thank you for last Saturday night, uh, allowing me to come and share in your birthday. And I'll talk to you later, and I love you. Bye-bye."

I regained control of my legs and headed to a meeting.

Hours later her words echo in my mind: *"—thanks for being our granddaughter, okay? Bye-bye."*

Okay, Grandma . . . and thank you for the 12,760 days we shared. I love you, I love you, I love you.

EPILOGUE

Thursday, December 24

I stopped the car and took a deep breath before getting out. The grass was wet. The buzz of chainsaws and wood chippers a few hundred yards away filled the air as tree trimmers went about their work.

I walked slowly. Cool air hit my face and the late-morning sun warmed my back.

Kneeling down my hand instinctively reached out and brushed stray grass clippings off the headstone. The edges of the raised letters still new and sharp stung my fingertips. It's been almost five months since I was here—then it was a mound of dirt covered with artificial turf, a deep hole swallowing a muted blue casket, an unsettled ache ripping open inside me—but today the scarred earth shows no sign of the violation . . . though my heart still gapes.

I've never gone to a cemetery alone. I've never gone for anything but a graveside service or unveiling. I never saw—or felt—the need to return. Until now. Now I had to go. I was drawn.

As I knelt and reread the words and dates I knew by heart I turned to Psalm 116. The words in verse 15 rang hollow when Uncie shared them at Grandma's graveside and memorial: "Precious in the sight of the LORD is the death of his saints." But today I sought refuge in the context. I read all nineteen verses, and how different it made it.

I flipped back a hundred psalms to find the phrase on her headstone—"in your presence there is fullness of joy"—and I read all eleven verses of that psalm, too.

Something shifted. A bit of the haze lifted.

"The lines have fallen for me in pleasant places; indeed, I have a beautiful inheritance" (16:6). "Gracious is the LORD, and righteous; our God is merciful. ...Return, O my soul, to your rest; for the LORD has dealt bountifully with you. For you have delivered my soul from death, my eyes from tears, my feet from stumbling; I will walk before the LORD in the land of the living. ...What shall I render to the LORD for all his benefits to me? ...I will offer to you the sacrifice of thanksgiving and call on the name of the LORD" (116:5, 7-8, 12, 17).

I am not done living.

I stood alone in a cemetery on Christmas Eve and felt more alive than ever. The cavernous grief is not gone. Grandma will not be at the table with us tonight. But my soul can rest. I have farther to walk. I have a beautiful inheritance. God is gracious and merciful. There is fullness of joy . . . joy and grief inseparably twined.

I am not done living. And neither is she. We're not living together for a while—but, oh, we are living.

AFTERWARD

I had a simple purpose as I chronicled my long goodbye to Grandma: Remember. Remember the good and the hard, the old stories and the new. Write it down so I could remember the feel of her hand in mine and the sight of her smile and the names of her childhood friends. And, most of all, capture her voice so I could hear her forever. I needed a record I could return to when the memories faded.

Writing kept me focused during a time I felt so lost. It reminded me to ask for old stories, to hold her memories for her and to explore the deep connection between us and between the generations. The actual written words were a raw document of the daily minutiae, a list of stories I wanted to circle back to, my own heartbreak and Grandma's family history lumped into one file, divided by the date and with a list of random reminders tacked on to the end. I never planned on sharing it with anyone. It was my own private refuge.

During the nineteen-month goodbye I also composed countless emails. A circle of friends—many of whom never met my grandma in person—faithfully prayed for our family. The emails were sporadic until Grandpa got sick June 12, 2015. From that day until Grandma died on July 26, 2015, I sent regular updates. Those emails formed a second, complementary record of the final six weeks of Grandma's life as we sat beside two bedsides and grappled with more unknowns than knowns.

The following pages have a different tone and feel than the preceding pages. They, too, were written in the moment, but they were written with a distinct audience and with the primary purpose of conveying information. They were a public record from the beginning as opposed to my private journal.

Friday, June 12: Please pray for my grandpa

Hi Friends,

I am with my grandma right now and will be spending the night here. But my grandpa was taken by ambulance to the hospital this afternoon and was admitted this evening.

He started feeling poorly yesterday (and fell four times in the past day) and saw his doctor this morning. He said the falls were due to the fever and that he had a serious throat infection. He sent him home with antibiotics and throat lozenges. While my mom and I were here (about 12:30) he was able to get the antibiotics down, but he was having a lot of trouble swallowing. After we left he began having trouble breathing and the paramedics transported him. My uncle has been with him at the hospital, and I am awaiting an update once my grandpa is settled in a room. His fever is very high, his sputum is brown and they can hear something in his lung(s). They've run numerous tests, but we have no results at this point.

Please pray for healing for my grandpa and for wisdom for us. Pray we would love both Grandma and Grandpa well right now and would know how to navigate these unexpected moments.

Thank you for your prayers.

Friday, June 12: Please pray for my grandpa – UPDATE

I just spoke with my mom: Grandpa has pneumonia. He is in a step up unit (or step down…seriously who names these things?) that is in between ICU and regular care. They anticipate him being in the hospital for a few days. He is receiving IV treatments tonight and will have a swallow test tomorrow. If he can't pass the swallow test, they will put a tube down his throat, and he will need to be awake/unsedated for that (not clear on the purpose of the tube, etc.). Not a lot of details, but it sounds like he's getting good care.

Pray for us to care for both my grandparents well. We know we are not walking alone, and that support means so much.

Saturday, June 13: Saturday Grandpa Update

Thanks so much for your prayers. Last night with my grandma went well (she slept great). My grandpa did not have such a good night. My mom and I spent some time with him late this morning and spoke with both his nurse and doctor. Basically his lungs look pretty good; but he did not pass the swallow test, he is still struggling to breathe, swallow, sleep, etc. The plan now is for them to insert a feeding tube (through the nose to the stomach) for food and some of the medicine that cannot be given through IV. He's exhausted and not excited about the tube, but he's game for anything that will get him home. He's worried about my grandma. But his spirits are pretty good. Before we left Mom prayed with/for him, and he seemed much comforted.

We are praying for the inflammation in his throat to go down, the infection to subside and for his health to be restored. The nurse said they really haven't seen much improvement in him yet other than his fever coming down somewhat.

My mom, aunt, cousins and I have worked out a night schedule to be with my grandma. So far she isn't aware that my grandpa isn't at home.

Please pray for the health of my grandparents, especially my grandpa's, right now. And please pray for us as we love and care for both of them. We know we are doing as well as we are because of God's grace and the prayers and support.

Sunday, June 14: Sunday Update on grandparents

Thank you for praying!

Short update: Grandpa is doing much better. Grandma is doing well. We covet your continued prayers!

Long update: Yesterday afternoon Grandpa asked to be given something to help him sleep. They gave him something and he slept. But once awake he became very confused. He pulled out the feeding tube (the one through the nose), repeatedly tried to get up/leave (he's now in soft restraints), was/is very unclear on where he is and didn't sleep last night. BUT before reinserting the tube today he was given another swallow test, and he passed! This was unexpected and huge, huge progress. I had a long conversation with the nurse today (I just missed the doctor). She is very encouraged. His confusion is clearing up a bit (though he tried to get up twice while Dad and I were there and was somewhat disoriented). The nurse thinks once he starts eating that will help flush the medication from his system and get his metabolism and immune system going. The echocardiogram results were great -- his heart is in very good condition. He's not retaining fluids. His voice sounded much better today, and his throat feels better. The antibiotics seem to be working very well. They are still calling it pneumonia, but the main issue really seems to be the throat, and it is clearly improving. The nurse thinks he will be moved tomorrow to a regular room and start on therapy (getting up to walk, etc.). His spirits are great, which is also a huge answer to prayer.

Grandma slept well last night and has eaten well (for her) yesterday and today. We discovered today she was/is supposed to be on antibiotics beginning on 6/11, and she didn't receive them on Friday or Saturday. I spoke with her hospice nurse today, and we got her back on the antibiotics today. She has not had the agitation issues and hasn't had to take anti-anxiety meds the past two or three days, though she did seem a bit hazy this afternoon while I was there. Hopefully the antibiotics will help her to feel better, too. She still seems unaware that Grandpa isn't home.

Specific requests: Eating would go well for Grandpa. His confusion will clear up. The infection/pneumonia will clear up entirely. He will sleep tonight. Grandma will continue to be comfortable and the antibiotics would work effectively. All of us would love and support them well and be able to get good information from and to their medical teams to best care for them. For those staying overnight with Grandma to get some sleep (that's not gone well so far). For wisdom for Mom and I in figuring out how and when we need to take time off work to care for them.

Thank you, thank you, thank you for praying with us and for loving my family so well!

Monday, June 15: Monday Update – not as good

Today was not quite as encouraging, but we press on and are grateful for each moment with each of my grandparents.

Grandma: slept well last night and ate well today. But she appears to be having some fluid retention (puffy hands, etc.) and some catheter issues. A nurse should be out this evening to check on both. She was alert and chatty, but fairly hard to understand when I was there. My cousin will be spending the night with her tonight. I believe my aunt will be there tomorrow when the doctor visits.

Grandpa: by last evening he was more confused and agitated. His Sunday night chest x-ray showed more cloudiness in his lungs; the pneumonia is worsening. Today his blood enzymes raised concerns about his heart, and when I was there after work they were about to do an ultrasound of his heart. He continues to be quite confused and needs to be restrained, which he does not like at all (it's a pretty cool vest thing that actually gives him a lot of motion, he just can't get up; he tries to get us to cut it off). On the plus side he is eating well and had physical therapy twice today. He slept well last night and slept a lot today, too.

Please pray for both of them to sleep well tonight and for their bodies to respond well to the medications they are taking. Pray too for us as we continue to try to advocate well for them and to understand as much as possible what everything means and what decisions need to be made. We're doing well, but it's a lot to process, stay on top of and keep clear communication between all of us.

Much thanks for your prayers and support!

Tuesday, June 16: Tuesday Update – better day so far

Thank you for praying. There are still more unknowns than knowns, but today has been better for both Grandpa and Grandma.

Grandpa: Mom and I talked with the nurse for a long time today and got a lot of helpful information. The pneumonia is still present. Last night's echocardiogram showed no real difference from Saturday's results, and that's good. There is some heart failure (and thus the fluid in his lungs), but all-in-all good for his age and health. There is some arrhythmia -- his days of regular coffee appear to be numbered as caffeine exacerbates the irregularity. The enzyme that was high on Sunday and higher yesterday is almost down to normal today. Great news. He had physical therapy this morning, and his oxygen levels dropped when he stood up, but they recovered when he laid back down. He seemed less confused today though his speech is still quite garbled (like talking with a mouth full of marbles -- the words/sentences all make sense and are correct, but he's hard to understand). He continues to sleep a lot. There is rumor he might be released to skilled nursing (within their retirement home) tomorrow, but we shall wait and see. He is still quite sick.

Grandma: The hospice nurse last night took care of the catheter issue but said Grandma is both dehydrated (despite the caregivers giving her lots of fluids) and retaining fluids. Her heart is working too hard with too little success. The nurse told Mom that Grandma is declining and declining rapidly. That said, today she was quite alert and communicative and though sometimes hard to understand her speech was less jumbled. The doctor agreed her heart is struggling but seemed hesitant to quantify her decline in any way. He said anything could happen at any time. The nurses and caregivers were able to reassess, verify and reorganize all her medications, so hopefully there won't be any more missed doses or questions on when she should or shouldn't be taking something.

All of us rest in the knowledge that God continues to be in control and sustain each of us through this time. What is unknown to us is fully known to Him. Thank you for praying with us.

Wednesday, June 17: Wednesday Update

Everything's so fluid! In the words of one of my former pastors, "Strap yourself in!" That's how the days are feeling. We hold the course of loving Grandpa and Grandma through the highs and lows as rapidly as they come. The good and bad nip at one another's heels.

Grandpa: He had a bad night last night. They had to significantly increase his oxygen (from low-flow to high-flow). He was still on the high-flow when I was there at 5 tonight. The chest x-ray and CT scan today showed no significant change in the pneumonia, which is still present in both lungs. This concerns me as that sounds like the pneumonia is not responding to the antibiotics. His voice is back in the very high pitch range and he has to pause for breath when he speaks. No physical therapy today. No appetite. BUT by this evening he had somehow gotten ahold of his cell phone and called Mom three times with requests/demands that show a marked improvement in his mental facilities (he made sense; he was very detailed; he recalled things from the day he got sick; he was stubborn and persistent -- classic Grandpa).

Grandma: She is the more stable of the two...go figure :) She timed a perfect one-liner and told me she was teasing Mom before promptly falling asleep. She had an uneventful day -- she ate, she slept, she had visitors, she was calm and relaxed. There was a little agitation this evening, but last I heard she was sleeping and will hopefully sleep well through the night. We got our lines crossed and none of us were there today when the hospice nurse was there (and if anyone got an update from her or the morning caregiver it hasn't made it to me yet).

Thank you for praying with us. It is a privilege to feel God's love for our family through you. Watching the kitchen staff come in to give Grandma a hug with her meal tray speaks as loudly as the faithful friends who visit Grandpa and leave notes of encouragement written on surgical masks. The family of God is amazing! We do not know what tonight or tomorrow holds, but we know He holds them and that is enough.

Thursday, June 18: Thursday Update – better news

Today there were good reports for both grandparents :)

Grandma: She had a rough night last night (waking up agitated and restless throughout the night), but today she seemed better. She ate decently and seemed comfortable.

Grandpa: Today's chest x-ray showed less cloudiness. The first solid sign the pneumonia is abating! As of the middle of the afternoon he was still on high-flow oxygen, and I assume he still is tonight. He is continuing to not want to eat (averaging about one meal a day). He is quite weak and couldn't handle standing up in physical therapy, but they got him sitting upright to do some things. We're grateful for every bit of progress.

My mom and uncle had lunch together, and they had a good talk about things that need to be done such as getting bills paid and working out a schedule for the nights with Grandma. Long story short and a lot of moving parts two of the caregivers volunteered to be available at night. Tonight and tomorrow night they are each taking a night, and then we'll reevaluate how Grandpa is and everything else.

Please continue to pray for wisdom and compassion for each of us and for good rest. I think everyone's feeling weary from the see-sawing news and emotions. We are blessed to have so many resources and people shouldering the responsibilities and privileges of loving our parents/grandparents. Please pray specifically for my grandpa to regain his appetite and strength, and pray for my grandma to feel well loved even in the moments we aren't with her.

Praying on.

Friday, June 19: Early update today

Pretty good news again today!

Grandma: She had a good night with the caregiver and seemed at ease today. She hadn't eaten as much, but her fluid levels were better. She was lucid and chatty with Mom and me. Grateful for sweet moments with her.

Grandpa: Physically he is improving. The pneumonia is clearing up. He is out of the restraint and back on low-flow oxygen, though the nurse said despite the less cumbersome delivery system he is still receiving the same high levels of oxygen. The biggest concern is how exhausted he is and that the doctors don't know what's causing it. The nurses are hoping to get doctor's orders to take him outside in the hope that being out of bed in sunshine, fresh air and with a change of scenery will help. During physical therapy today he took three steps but then couldn't do any more. He ate a little bit more than yesterday, and hopefully he'll eat dinner tonight. He was more conversant and easier to understand although he couldn't keep his eyes open; they were closed most of the time we were there. He knows he has a long road ahead of him, and we did talk a little about what that might look like (though the nurse said the doctors are not yet talking about releasing him).

Please pray for Grandpa to continue to get stronger and for him to be released at the exact right time. Pray for wisdom in knowing when and how to proceed with arrangements for Grandma now and for both of them when he is released.

Thank you for your prayers. If things continue to hold steady, I will probably stop the daily updates, but I do appreciate your prayers and support. As things progress I'll be sure to let you know. Thank you for praying with and for us through this!

Sunday, June 21: Grandpa's out of the hospital

My grandpa was discharged late this afternoon! He is technically in the same building as my grandma now (she's in their apartment in the independent living area with 24-hr caregivers; he's in skilled nursing for rehab). Yesterday he was able to walk maybe twenty steps with a walker and "two guys" as he put it. I was with him at the hospital today, and he said he'd eaten a good breakfast and promised to eat all his lunch that was being delivered as I left. He is still tired and has no appetite, but he is beginning to seem more like himself (the fight is definitely coming back).

Yesterday and today he repeatedly told me he doesn't think he'll ever see my grandma again. My goal tomorrow is to arrange with skilled nursing for him to be wheeled to the apartment to see her. I assured him today that I had just come from seeing her and had a good chat with her and that she is being well cared for.

Please pray for him to continue to progress and heal well. And please pray specifically that he will be able to go visit my grandma in the next day or two. She seems stable for now, but we don't know what each day will look like.

Also, my parents were able to leave this morning for their annual vacation to Hume Lake. They will return at a moment's notice, but please pray for them to be able to stay for most or all of the week. This has been a hard week on top of a long few months, and I'm so glad they were able to go to a place they both love and that renews them! Pray for me to be extra attentive to my grandparents while my parents are gone.

Thank you for your continued prayers!

Tuesday, June 23: Good Tuesday Update

It has been a good couple days for both grandparents!

Grandpa: Yesterday was mostly assessments and paperwork. On a scale of 0-10, he said he was a three but couldn't explain what that meant. Today when I arrived he immediately asked me to go to the apartment and get him clothes. When he arrived at therapy this morning he was stunned to see everyone else dressed, which made him self-conscious about his hospital gown (yesterday he did not want clothes when I offered). He admitted therapy was hard and wore him out, but he seemed pleased with how it had gone. My uncle and I got the chance to talk with his nurse, get a speech therapy update and meet with his physical therapist. It looks like a minimum of two weeks in skilled nursing (based on speech therapy which is "swallow training" to try to make sure there's no more food/liquid aspiration). After nearly an hour of occupational therapy the physical therapist worked with him for 75 minutes and said she thinks they'll be able to begin weaning him off the oxygen within days and that he is already making progress strength wise but has a long way to go. And, we got the doctor's note allowing Grandpa to go visit Grandma! At this point my uncle is the only one allowed to take him, so I'm not sure when that will be, maybe Thursday. Very encouraging news all the way around.

Grandma: She continues to be alert and talkative. She spent a solid five minutes tonight telling me about a very judgmental man who she thinks might be a little gentler now, but he is a judgmental man who judges. I have no idea whom (if anyone) she was talking about…possibly the doctor who visited this afternoon. I'm not sure she knew me today, but she seemed very comfortable and content, and for that I am grateful.

Thank you, thank you for your prayers. They mean so much. Each day is a gift, and I am trying to treasure them all.

Saturday, June 27: Good Grandparents Update

Short update: Multiple good days in a row--we're all so grateful!! Yesterday (Friday) was a good, good day.

Long update: Wednesday Grandpa had a chest x-ray. On Thursday the speech therapist told him the results were good. I assumed this was pneumonia related, but she explained it had to do with ensuring he had not aspirated any food or liquid since he'd been released from the hospital. The x-ray was good. The visual assessments were good. He's satisfactorily using the swallow tips and techniques. So on Friday a second therapist signed off, and he's completed his speech therapy (swallow training) in half the anticipated time. He's a determined man.

Also on Friday he was able to visit my grandma. The caregiver said he was so happy he cried. Today he said how great she looked and how good the time was. An absolute answer to prayer for him/them to get that time! (The downside is he's eager to go back, but the nurse warned us that for insurance purposes we need to be careful about how often he goes lest they decide the outings mean he's too healthy for skilled nursing.)

In general, he's more and more himself each day. He's spending much more time awake and out of bed (sitting up in a wheelchair). He wants to get better so badly he's doing his seated and reclined physical therapy exercises on his own a few extra times a day. He's doing a surprisingly good job of following the rules and not doing things he's not supposed to do (getting up unattended, etc.). Well, he's mostly doing a good job, I pointed out he wasn't using his oxygen today, and he waved his hand at it and said it was in the way when he was rolling (a foot and a half) to the cupboard. Apparently it remained in the way once he was finished...

He's eating more though he doesn't have much of an appetite. He says they send him way too much food--it's about half of what he used to eat at a meal. The chef has begun adding surprise treats to his tray (like a side of bread and butter pickles) that he knows my grandpa likes. It's a shame my grandparents aren't loved :)

And sweet Grandma continues to amaze us. Today she was asleep and did not wake up during our visit, but generally she was awake and alert when I visited each day this week. The caregivers are dressing her in new, cute tops they've brought her (ones she would never have agreed to wear of her own free will) and supplement her typical meals with watermelon and other things they bring in to boost her calories and fluids. It is touching to see how protective they are of her and how invested in her care they are. They stay on top of every detail and are quick to call in the hospice nurse if they think anything is even slightly abnormal.

My parents arrived home yesterday. They had a great time away, and they're glad to be home (and I'm glad for additional people back in the visiting and information-gathering rotation).

Thank you, thank you for praying with and for us. There are no words to express our gratitude at being loved and supported so well through the steep descents and miraculous ascents of the sixteen days since Grandpa got sick and the almost eighteen months since Grandma first got sick. We are blessed beyond measure!

Saturday, July 11: Saturday (7/11) Grandparents Update

This has been a week of changes for both grandparents. I am reminded on a daily (hourly?) basis of the truth of Proverbs 19:1 as we have many plans (or assumptions) but it is God's purpose that prevails every time. Most of the changes are ultimately in my grandparents' best interest, and even what I had hoped for to a large degree; but at the same time more and more control and dignity seems to be stripped away from them in the process. That is hard to witness and participate in.

Brief Update

Yesterday (7/10) my grandpa was moved to a new room in skilled nursing, and my grandma was then moved to join him. He continues therapy and will at some point be able to move back to their apartment or (more likely) to assisted living. My grandma will remain in skilled nursing until she goes home to heaven.

Longer Update

My grandpa is improving, but he is not making the progress his team (therapists, doctor, nurses, unit directors at the facility, etc.) anticipated. I believe a significant reason for his apparent slow progress is that the team and my grandpa may not have an accurate understanding of what his physical condition was prior to contracting pneumonia. Due to his neuropathy and spinal stenosis his balance had already deteriorated beyond what he acknowledged. I think their target for rehab is higher than his pre-illness reality, so while he has 1.5-3 hours of therapy a day and works very hard, his balance and strength is never going to be what they are hoping for. They will continue to reevaluate his progress on a weekly basis until it is determined he has either reached his goal and can go home or reached the maximum level of ability short of his goal and needs to transition to assisted living.

In addition to the slower gains physically my grandpa also seems to be having some mental confusion (sundowners, perhaps?) and to be getting discouraged. In the assessment meeting on Thursday when he found out he wasn't being released from skilled nursing, he also heard that while the goal is to return to independent living (his apartment), the reality might be transitioning to assisted living instead. Between that and feeling that these decisions are now being made for him instead of with him, my mom and I are sensing a downturn in his spirit and a feeling of defeat. He is a planner, and this is beyond even his contingency plans.

My grandma continues to baffle everyone and is medically stable. However, the move yesterday was difficult on her (physically it was uncomfortable, mentally/emotionally it was confusing). We aren't sure whom she recognizes or to what degree, but this move means a revolving door of RNs/CNAs/LVNs caring for her and even in the time I was with her yesterday during the move, that appeared to be hard for her. She never asks for anything and cannot do anything for herself, so while I am grateful for the increased medical support, I am concerned that her food and fluid intake will decrease without caregivers constantly at her side with whom she is familiar and who patiently and compassionately tend to her. I believe this was the right move in many ways, but I also believe this will hasten her home going and make her final days less comfortable and more bewildering.

These moves were done with good and right intentions--and needed to happen--yet I feel a sense of finality and sadness. My grandparents are blessed with friends who visit them faithfully, but it is hard to watch their world shrink so dramatically so quickly.

Please pray for us to love them well and to be thoughtful and creative in honoring their dignity and desires while also advocating well for the best and wisest care for them.

Your prayers, concern and support mean far more than I can say.

Friday, July 24: News on my grandparents

My cousin and I spent some time with my grandparents today. The doctor said Tuesday he noticed a marked decline in my grandma between last week and this week. That decline has only accelerated the last few days. Yesterday afternoon I noticed the sound of her breathing had changed. By last night her ability to swallow had decreased. She ran a fever overnight, and it seemed to be back this afternoon. Today a breathing treatment helped some, but the hospice nurse explained to us that her organs are beginning to shut down. The nurse was very gracious and spent a lot of time with my cousin and me. My grandma can hear us, but her ability to communicate is very minimal. For about a week she has clearly been in pain, and while today she did not seem to be hurting, it was hard to watch her struggle to breathe. It is hard to be helpless.

My grandpa is doing all right. They are still together, and that is good for both of them. I hope.

Please pray for her not to be in pain and for her to be safely home soon. And pray for us, please.

Sunday, July 26: Sunday Update on Grandma

Thank you for your prayers this weekend. Friday night Grandma slipped into a coma. The pain seems to be gone, and she has been peaceful most of the time. Her breathing continues to be labored and somewhat erratic. She has not had food or water since Friday morning (or Thursday night…a bit unclear). A nurse told my uncle this afternoon that we are looking at two or three days. While that seems much more likely with the coma and lack of fluids, we know the timing has never been for us to know, so we wait for His timing.

The emotions are unpredictable for each of us, but we are so grateful for the support we receive from one another and our amazing extended family of friends.

Much love and gratitude.

Monday, July 27: Grandma's Final Update

Thank you, friends, for your prayers. Shortly before midnight last night Grandma exhaled on earth and inhaled in heaven. She is finally home with Jesus. I spent the morning with my grandpa, my mom and my uncle. There were tears, and there was laughter -- I expect much more of both in the hours, days and weeks to come. We've made initial plans and are dealing with many details that will be solidified in the next few days. I would appreciate your continued prayers as there are many more phone calls and decisions to be made.

ABOUT THE AUTHOR

Kristen Hartman is the third born of Maxine Dagen's only daughter Joanne and the middle of her favorite five grandchildren. She has been the caretaker and chronicler of Maxine's stories for years—a joy and responsibility that was accelerated when the family realized their mother, grandmother and great-grandmother was failing. Short pieces about her grandma have appeared on Kristen's blog, Looking Through Me, and thereby have endeared her grandma even to people who never met her (though wish they had). This is not only the story of a life well-lived, but of the granddaughter who finds her roots therein.

Made in the USA
San Bernardino, CA
27 January 2017